THE SOURCES
OF
ENGLISH LITERATURE

THE

SOURCES OF ENGLISH LITERATURE

A BIBLIOGRAPHICAL GUIDE FOR STUDENTS

Sandars Lectures 1926

by

ARUNDELL ESDAILE, M.A.

of the British Museum
Sometime Scholar of Magdalene College

CAMBRIDGE

AT THE UNIVERSITY PRESS

1929

CAMBRIDGE UNIVERSITY PRESS
Cambridge, New York, Melbourne, Madrid, Cape Town,
Singapore, São Paulo, Delhi, Mexico City

Cambridge University Press
The Edinburgh Building, Cambridge CB2 8RU, UK

Published in the United States of America by Cambridge University Press, New York

www.cambridge.org
Information on this title: www.cambridge.org/9781107626386

First Edition 1928
Reprinted with corrections 1929
First published 1929
First paperback edition 2013

A catalogue record for this publication is available from the British Library

ISBN 978-1-107-62638-6 Paperback

To

A. W. POLLARD
MAGISTRO
DISCIPULUS

NOTE

I have revised these lectures, and included references to some publications of 1927.

My thanks are due to Mr Seymour de Ricci, who gave me some notes on private book-collectors.

A.E.

CONTENTS

vii

THE SOURCES
OF
ENGLISH LITERATURE

Elected by my University to follow in this Readership the company of the greatest bibliographers of
this generation and the last—among them our late
Librarian, through whom the light lit by Henry
Bradshaw was passed on, Gordon Duff, who received it from him, and who not only in his Sandars
lectures but in his bequest acknowledged his debt
to Cambridge, and Mr Alfred Pollard, from whom
I also have imbibed the tradition—I must begin by
explaining why, unlike them, I do not propose to
detail the results of some specific piece of bibliographical research, and why it is not the profane,
but the initiate, to whom I would cry *procul, o
procul.*

While still turning about in the English books of
the later seventeenth century, at which I was then
working in view of the handlist of that period
which is to be the next in the Museum's series of
special catalogues, and following two or three lines,
rather uncertain which to take, I was removed
from my peaceful province to one in which there
is no peace, and (what is worse) no books, other
than those which enshrine minutes and official

3

correspondence. For a time, exactly fulfilling the description of Issachar as "a strong ass couching between two burdens", I doubted whether I ought not to resign the Readership. But time was growing short, and I reflected that if I gave up the idea of embodying new research, I might yet fulfil the intentions expressed by Mr Sandars in his foundation of this Readership.

The function of Universities in promoting research and the disinterested addition to knowledge is normally that one of their functions which is most easily neglected. But in this particular field it is the reverse. The Sandars lectures as a series represent a massive body of profound and original learning. But to profit by them, their hearers must have already had not only much instruction, but much practical experience of similar researches. There seemed therefore to be room for a year in which these lectures should be addressed, not to palaeographers or palaeotypographers but to novices, to mere readers of books, not to College Librarians but to undergraduates. Having for several years taught the first elements of bibliography in the School of Librarianship at University College, London—a School of a kind, let me add, of which the first to be founded should have been founded not at a younger University, but at Cambridge—it seemed that I might well attempt "things unattempted yet" in this place. Some

4

small part indeed of the material I shall give you in these lectures formed part of lectures of different scope given in that School, and it is to the excellent notes of a member of my class that I owe the sole record of them—this being, doubtless, the only point in which I resemble Aristotle and St Thomas Aquinas.

Even the elements of bibliography are a very large and diverse field; and it remained to select some branch of it, within my own competence and of use to as many of you as might be. The choice was easy. We have here a large and distinguished School of English; much of my experience has been gained in the arduous task of filling up the gaps in the Museum's collection of English books of the sixteenth, seventeenth, and eighteenth centuries. The sources of the bibliography of English literature then are my subject.

THE NEED OF BIBLIOGRAPHY

It is not at all a new observation that as mathematics are the grammar of physical science, so bibliography is the grammar of what used to be called book-learning, the science which is to be drawn from the written or printed word. And this is peculiarly true of the historical study of literature, for in that study the exact words of an author are,

5

as in no other, vital. Of rival texts you must decide which is the true one, that is, often, but not always, the earliest; and errors and imperfections in the text chosen you have to explain in ways not inconsistent with the methods of book production of the time.

All of you, as professed students of English literature, will have to do this; but some of you will no doubt edit early authors, and you will find that a good editor is only a good student putting his principles into practice, and that every good student is a good editor *in posse*. The knowledge at the base of the student's and the editor's work alike must be a knowledge, first of the author's own writings; of the editions or sources chosen so that the true text is available, and arranged in order of appearance so that his development may be clearly traced; and also a knowledge of the writings of his time. All this cannot exist without bibliography. Behind every editor stands a bibliographer, and according to the work of the latter will the work of the former be; obviously the two heads should wear the same hat. Before our editor-bibliographer can choose his texts, he must find them. Moreover, when he has in his hand a copy of an original edition, he may well have some doubt of its perfection when he collates it, which only another copy, or even other copies, can set at rest. Again, scholars are now realising more and more that in the days of the cumbrous and slowly working hand-

press it was an easy and frequent matter to alter
the pages (called by the printer the "forme") when
only partly printed off. The result is that two copies
of the same edition of the same book may reveal
important variations.

An instance of this which has recently (because
of the high price paid) attracted a good deal of
public attention is that of the first edition of the
Pilgrim's Progress, pt 1, 1678. Five perfect copies
are known. There may of course be more—but so
far no more have appeared; and the scores that
have been sent to the Museum by their sanguine
owners since the sale in 1926 of Mr Warner's
copy have all been of the nineteenth century; one
was authenticated (by letter) as the first edition,
since it contained "a photo of Bunyan opposite the
front page". Well, in two of these copies the space
below the "Finis" is occupied by five lines of
errata, obviously discovered after the printing-off
of the earlier sheets they refer to, and during the
printing-off of the last sheet. They certainly represent what Bunyan wrote; and any editor who
reprinted from one of the other three copies without collating one of these and incorporating the
corrections, would be missing a point.

Before I leave this matter I will give you one
more instance, this time from a French and not
from an English book, one which has, so far as
I know, not been noted by bibliographers.

7

Ordinary copies of the "Histoire de Barbarie et de ses Corsaires, par le R. P. F. Pierre Dan, Ministre et Supérieur du Couvent de la Ste Trinité... Bachelier en Théologie", Paris, 1637, 4°, have the last leaf of Book 2, p. 251 and blank (sig. Ii 2), a cancelling leaf, giving Dan's account of Berber marriage customs. There is a copy of the book in this, the ordinary state, in King George III's Library (147. b. 18). There is in the Museum another copy, in the Old Royal Library, bound in red Turkey morocco with Charles II's cypher (C. 80. a. 2). In this copy the original cancelled leaf remains in its place; the scissor slit, the signal to the binder to cancel it, was ignored, as it was made in the middle instead of at the foot of the leaf. The cancelling text is found printed on the blank last leaf of the book, thus economising press-work. The original text of p. 251 reveals a surprising variation. It contains a sentence, which the author discovered after that sheet, but before the last, was printed off. The newly married Corsair bride, he says, "ne sort point du logis, disant qu'elle porte le dueil de sa virginité, qu'elle suit l'exemple de la fille de Iephté, qui après auoir perdu la sienne, courut toute désolée les montagnes de Iudée, & qu'elle l'imiteroit tres volontiers en ce poinct-là, n'estoit l'apprehension qu'elle a des lyons, & des autres bestes cruelles & dangereuses".

The whole of this, after "porte le dueil de sa

8

virginité ", is omitted in the King's Library copy.
Now, one does not have to be a Reverend Father
Superior to perceive that there is something wrong
about this version of the story of the Daughter of
Jephtha. And in fact, on referring to Judges xi. 38
in the Vulgate and in the French Bible, you will
find that "deflevit virginitatem suam per illos
montes"—"elle ploroit sa virginité ès montagnes".
She lamented her virginity on the mountains, not,
of course, because she had lost it, which she had
not, but because she was not to lose it, nor to be
a mother in Israel. The reverend author must
have been eager to cover up his absurd mistake
in time; but the negligence of a binder has, after
nearly three centuries, betrayed his secret.

Now if you had been reprinting Dan on the
Barbary Corsairs, and supposing that you had an
ordinary copy, in the corrected state, on finding
this leaf to be a cancel you would instantly have
had to set out to find all the other copies available,
until you had traced one that contained the un-
corrected original leaf. My hunt was short; but it
might have been long. Success has not yet attended
that for a copy of Boswell's *Tour to the Hebrides* with
the original leaf containing the first version of the
account of Sir Alexander Macdonald's want of hos-
pitality. When one reads the second, which in its
turn was toned down (it is said under threat of the
horsewhip) for the second edition, one wonders what

9

the first can possibly have been. Of every edition of the sixteenth, seventeenth, and eighteenth centuries several copies should be collated; if one only finds a thrifty author like Munday dedicating different copies of the same book to different patrons, one learns some fact worth knowing, as well as picking up a little ill-natured amusement by the way.

But to trace other copies of a known book, just as to gather records of unknown books, requires a repertory of all English books of the period in hand. Where does such a list exist? It is safe to say, after 1640 and till the other day outside the quarter of a century before 1500, nowhere. The best we can do is to know what bibliographies and catalogues exist, and to that knowledge I hope to provide you with some introduction.

WORLD BIBLIOGRAPHY

There are a sort of projectors, as Swift would term them, who call for a complete bibliography of the world's literature. They are, indeed, more modest than those (they really existed, if they do not still exist) who called for a single detailed index of all printed matter, wherever or whenever produced. When the promoters of these schemes descend from Laputa, a little conversation with bibliographers who live and work on the mere

surface of this planet will sober their bibliographical intoxication.

Yet even at the risk of swamping not only the
sacred poets with themselves, but ourselves with the
journalists and the pot-boilers, it would undoubtedly be a very fine thing to have a world list of
books and printed pieces. But there must be some
thirty million in existence—perhaps more; a hundred years ago the known products of the first
half-century of printing amounted to about 16,000;
to-day twice as many are known, and every year
a few more crop up in dealers' lists. The Museum
Catalogue alone contains an average of 1000
English books dating from every year between
1641 and 1700, and it is only for the first third of
this period that, by the exertions of George
Thomason, it has a really large proportion of the
actual output. There were produced in England
last year (of the aristocracy of books which are
entered in the English Catalogue) 13,202 works; in
France of the similar class, entered in the *Biblio-
graphie de la France*, 8464 in 1924; but the French
list is not so representative as the English, not
nearly so representative as the German; the new
loi de dépôt of 1925 will probably swell the annual
list very largely. For Germany, Austria and
Switzerland, there were entered in Hinrichs'
Halbjahrskatalog of 1925, about 35,000. (The
German figures include parts of serials, etc.) The

British Museum records the accession of 36,506 books and pamphlets, excluding all serials, journals, newspapers, maps and music, but including some thousands of foreign books.

The fully developed scheme is a crowning achievement for a leisured, eclectic age, an Age of the Antonines; and before we approach fruition that age may have been resolved afresh out of repose and recollection into struggle and new creation. But till then we do well, while nourishing a sense of proportion and of the possible, to work towards a national contribution to this larger ideal. You at least are not in doubt about the value of English literature; nor am I.

To you and to me it is a matter of importance that English books should be known, recorded and collected in national and University libraries where we can study them.

Nor do we suppose that the books worthy of our study are merely the great books, shining mountain peaks divided by dark and horrid gulfs. The bibliography of English literature that is to serve students will not merely record the best sellers of the auction room, the books that no millionaire's library is complete without, such as the four folios of Shakespeare and the Kilmarnock Burns; these are great books indeed, but we are also concerned with books that are not, like these, *idola fori*. A dull volume of controversial theology may make a

vital allusion, even if only by way of condemn-
ation, to a great author; many such are to be found
in the Shakespeare and Chaucer allusion books.
Or it may be a book that helped to form his ideas,
or one which he made fun of. Or its contents may
be totally null and negligible, and its author as
though he had not been born, yet peculiarities in
its printing may throw light on similar peculiarities
in the printing of books that do matter; the types,
the ornaments, the printer's device, the progressive
cracks or wormholes in the woodcuts used in both,
taken together with a signed and dated title-page
or colophon in the unimportant book, may establish
the date and the authority of the masterpiece. I do
no more now than allude to these uses of insignificant books; because you can find in Dr McKerrow's
" Notes on Bibliographical Evidence " (*Bibliographical Society's Transactions*, vol. xii—enlarged
edition now published, 1927) a masterly analysis
of all this part of bibliographical method, especially
as applied to English books of the sixteenth and
early seventeenth centuries. I mention them in
order to justify ourselves in including the rank and
file of books in bibliographies of a national literature. The same argument justifies the production of
lists of the products of particular periods and also of
particular presses. I may be excused in Cambridge
for making special mention (I shall have of course
to mention it again in its proper place) of the

remarkable catalogue of the English books printed before 1640 in our University Library, compiled now some twenty years ago by our regretted friend Charles Sayle; for it is a palmary example of the service a catalogue drawn up on these lines can perform; it has indeed since its publication been the chief authority for the presses which were at work in England between 1556 and 1640.

MANUSCRIPTS

While dwelling, in the course of these preliminary remarks, on the need for the study of printing by literary historians, I must add a word to exonerate myself from the charge of ignoring manuscripts. I do nothing of the kind. For the first seven hundred years of our literature the sources are all manuscript; and the written book is as much a book as the most standardised offspring of the steam press, and equally the material of bibliography; the methods by which both are collated and described, dated and placed, are in principle the same. But I have spent my life in a library so great that it is divided sharply into departments of printed books and of manuscripts; and being a printed-book man I am *ex hypothesi* ignorant of manuscripts. I must therefore leave it to some successor in this place to expound with knowledge, as I cannot, the work which has been done towards a complete corpus of bibliographical information as to the surviving manuscript volumes in which Old and Middle English literature have come down to us, and also the chief literary manuscripts of the age of print. He will shew what part English works played in monastic and collegiate libraries; he will trace for you the rise in the sixteenth century of the spirit of patriotism, and the resulting interest in the early chronicles of England; the attempts at a complete bibliography of English authors by Leland, Bale and Pits; the beginnings of the study of Old English by Archbishop Parker and his circle, whose monument is the Library of Corpus; the accumulation of historical material by Cotton, the development of the Royal Library and the gathering of these with the Harleian manuscripts into the British Museum; the attempt at a collective series of catalogues of Old English manuscripts by Humphrey Wanley. He will shew how the accumulating mass of sources and the growing ease of tracing them in catalogues gradually made possible the scientific editing of such a classic as Chaucer (for whose text the printed editions are quite secondary), from Caxton, through William Thynne, Speght, Urry, Tyrwhitt, and others, down to Skeat, and how, not content even with Skeat, a body of Chaucerians in the United States, headed by Professor Manly, is to-day gathering complete photostat reproductions of all the seventy-five or so surviving manuscripts of the *Canterbury Tales*, with the intention of producing, if possible, a definitive edition. Were I he, I would discuss the possibility of producing a comprehensive catalogue—or perhaps summary list, with references to full catalogues—of all English literary manuscripts in accessible libraries, and outline the steps to be taken towards that end.

A complete bibliography of all manuscripts in British libraries is doubtless a task of enormous complexity; nor would the result justify the labour, since the material would be so diverse. But that a summary bibliography of a limited class, such as I suggest, is not impossible, may be inferred from the fact that Professor and Mrs Charles Singer are well on in a bibliography of another such class, mediaeval scientific manuscripts of English origin. Their list is expected to contain between 30,000 and 40,000 articles. It would be difficult to guess the number of extant Old and Middle English literary manuscripts, but it can hardly be less. I am not ignorantly desiderating a work of impossible dimensions and doubtful utility. It is a possible if not immediate task for co-operative palaeographers. No doubt there is much more preliminary spadework to do. The British Museum's manuscripts, for example, are catalogued by the collections they belong to. Some of these separate catalogues are old and on our standards unscientific (it is said that in one of them a manuscript is cautiously dated "ni fallor, saeculo tertiodecimo, quartodecimo vel quintodecimo"); and until they can be brought up to a modern standard, no adequate comprehensive class-lists can well be produced. It is worth while and of good augury to remind ourselves that up to 1880 the presence of a printed book in the Museum Library could in the same way only be ascertained by search in three different catalogues, that of the Main Library (which included the old Royal Library and acquisitions by purchase, copyright and gift), that of King George III's Library (called, in distinction from the Old Royal, the King's), and that of the Grenville Library, bequeathed in the middle of the nineteenth century. These two latter catalogues were both large, and both abounded in rare English books. The amalgamation of the whole into a single printed and published catalogue seems to us obvious, and the previous age an age of darkness.

Elsewhere there is a large body of work to go upon. Here in Cambridge we can look the world in the face, for there can be few manuscripts in our libraries that have not been exactly described in published catalogues, for the most part by Dr Montague Rhodes James. Oxford has had the work of H. O. Coxe, Mr Falconer Madan and others at the Bodleian, and is producing just what the Museum lacks, a comprehensive summary catalogue of all the collections; but the manuscripts in Oxford college libraries are by no means so well catalogued. Many cathedral and collegiate libraries elsewhere, on the other hand, have been adequately catalogued, and so have some private collections. To get a more or less rapid conspectus of what there is to be dealt with I will only refer you to three or four easily accessible repertories, such as Wanley's list of Old English MSS. in Hickes's *Thesaurus*, vol. II, 1705, and that (to leap a couple of centuries) by Professor Carleton Brown, recording and analysing the contents of all manuscripts containing English religious verse of the thirteenth, fourteenth and fifteenth centuries, from unique pieces to the *Prick of Conscience*, which is found in 99 surviving copies. The contents-table of this work is an excellent handy list of libraries likely to contain other English manuscripts. Then there is Sir Edmund Chambers's *Mediaeval Stage* (1903), with its full list of dramatic texts; Mr C. L. Kingsford's *English Historical Literature of the Fifteenth Century*; the Reports and Appendices of the Historical Manuscripts Commission; (Gross's *Sources and Literature of English History* enters only printed texts, but gives a very useful bibliography of catalogues of manuscripts); Professor J. E. Wells's *Manual of*

Middle English Writings, to 1400 (Professor Wells has a similar manual for the fifteenth century in preparation); the introductions to the many volumes of the E.E.T.S. and the Chaucer Society; and for Chaucer himself the splendid "topical" bibliography (*Chaucer: a bibliographical manual*) by Miss E. P. Hammond. I can only hope that in my ignorance I have not omitted the most important.

All these afford, as you can see, a sound basis for an estimate of the mass of material and of the methods needed to deal with it. But in throwing out these hints and scraps I am only guarding myself, and perhaps also the less experienced of you, from the narrowness incidental to the bibliographer for whom a book has always in practice meant a book in print. I will turn to my real matter, the making of the bibliographies of printed editions which are contributions to the complete record of English books.

It would be possible, and rather attractive, to begin with the earliest to be produced, let us say from James's Bodleian Catalogue of 1605, and to work forwards, shewing the development of knowledge and method, till we come to the latest product of our bibliographical societies. But I believe that you will find more profit if I rather divide them into classes, and describe and rapidly discuss the chief specimens of each.

These classes are:

I. General bibliographies.
II. General catalogues of the large libraries of deposit and research.
III. Guides for book collectors, and dictionaries of rare books.
IV. Bibliographies of current literature made by the book-trade.
V. General lists of the products of particular periods.
VI. Lists of the products of particular provinces, counties, localities or universities.
VII. Lists of works in particular literary classes or forms.
VIII. Lists of the works of members of religious bodies.
IX. Bibliographies of single authors.
X. Dictionaries of anonyma and pseudonyma.
XI. Catalogues of private libraries; indexes of book sales.
XII. Lists of bibliographies.

GENERAL BIBLIOGRAPHIES

The first class, the general bibliography, is like the mammoth, extinct. It was a faint afterglow of the time when a scholar could aim at being a *doctor universalis*. We are more sober and more humble

now. There are, however, one or two of these
great books which are still used. The earliest list
of English-printed books is that by Andrew
Maunsell, a London bookseller. The first two
parts of his *Catalogue of English Printed Books*, the
first dealing with Divinity and the second with
"The Sciences Mathematicall, as Arithmetick,
Geometrie, Astronomie, Astrologie, Musick, the
Arte of Warre and Nauigation, and also of Physick
and Surgery", appeared in 1595. The third and
last part was never published, for Maunsell died
before the end of 1596. It was to have been "of
Humanity", and in it the author says, "I shall
have occasion to shew what we have in our owne
tongue, of Gramer, Logick, Rethoricke, Lawe,
Historie, Poetrie, Policie, etc., which will for the
most part concerne matters of Delight and Pleasure." How valuable would this part have been
to us! But Maunsell considered the other two the
necessary parts, and postponed this to them. When
we remember that the books were nearly contemporary, this does not seem so unimaginative as
at first sight. The titles are arranged as in a
subject-index. If we look into them we find more
approximation to modern exactness and fulness
than in many later bibliographers; he gives
printer and size, as well as date. In his divinity
section he announces one prudent but regrettable
limitation: "The auncient Popish bookes that have

been Printed heere I have inserted among the rest, but the Bookes written by the fugitive Papistes, as also those that are written against the present Government, I do not thinke meete for me to meddle withall." Maunsell calls his achievement "a most tiresome businesse", and all bibliographers will at times agree with him; but he adds that there is also "a blessing upon the labours undertaken in our poor estate". Let us agree with this too, and add that there are also "matters of Delight and Pleasure". Someone should go through his book, and note everything which is not recorded in the catalogues of English books to 1640, of which more in their place.

Michel Maittaire, who worked in England in the early part of the eighteenth century, amongst his other labours sharing the cataloguing of the Harleian printed books for Osborne the bookseller with William Oldys and the young Samuel Johnson, is perhaps the best known of the universal bibliographers. He is one of the early historians of typography, and his great work, *Annales artis typographicae*, is compiled, as the title implies, in chronological form, beginning with the period to 1500; it was published in 1719, and carried on to 1664 in later volumes published up to 1741. An index of towns and printers concludes the whole.

Maittaire is international, and English books

play an inconspicuous part in his *Annales*. English books, on the other hand, are the main store of the last of this giant race before the flood of modern book-production. Robert Watt was a Scottish doctor, who from his early student days began to collect and record books useful to medical students—for whom there was practically no guide to the literature they wanted—and, gradually developing his scheme to embrace foreign literature, ancient and modern, died under the weight of it in 1819, when the printing had begun. His great work was published in 1824, and was entitled *Bibliotheca Britannica, or a general index to British and foreign literature*. The word British is an outcrop, as it were, of an older stratum of the scheme, on which the foreign element was superimposed. But it is in fact the British part of it which has value to-day, and makes Watt the first alternative to the catalogues of the greatest libraries for establishing the existence of English books, especially the obscure books of the century and a half before his time. His critical remarks are careful and based on the best authority available to him. We must of course not expect more detail than short title, date and place, and a page of Watt is a repulsive object to the eye, being a tight mass of small type, owing nothing of such clearness as it possesses to the typographer's art. The book is divided into two parts, authors and subjects;

23

anonymous works must be looked for under their subject. Watt's great achievement is one of the largest of the many which bibliography owes to that constantly recurring type, the scholar physician.

There are two or three modern works which may be regarded as bringing up the rear of this class.

I hesitate to mention the *Dictionary of English Literature* (1859–91), by S. A. Allibone. Of course authors of the half-century after Watt may be found in it; but this is the period of the developed current trade bibliographies, both in England and America, and except for ready reference (if you are prepared to face the worse than superfluous addition of uncritical praises of authors, extracted from obscure reviews) there is not much use to be made of it.

There are also two large co-operative works which you all know, the bibliographies in which amount to very considerable bodies of titles to our purpose. The first is the *Dictionary of National Biography*; the second is the *Cambridge History of English Literature*. The defect of co-operative work is very apparent in both; the best bibliographies, such as Wheatley's of Dryden or Miss Spurgeon's of William Law and the English Mystics in the *Cambridge History*, could hardly be improved; but on the other hand, some, not to be named, are

24

deplorable, and many in the *Dictionary of National Biography* are copied straight from the Museum Catalogue, with no attempt at filling the gaps, perhaps in the pathetic belief that there are none.

GENERAL CATALOGUES OF
GREAT LIBRARIES

In the time of Watt the great national and University libraries were not only actually smaller (by the absence of all that has since appeared) but also relatively smaller than they are to-day; and by no means all of them had complete catalogues. Their catalogues however, whether in published form or as kept up to date in the libraries themselves and easily consulted, are now the main record of English books. Let us hastily run through them, ignoring the older catalogues they superseded, which are of no interest to-day, except for library history or settling some doubtful point of provenance.

The unification of the King's and General Library Catalogues of the Museum was the stepping stone to the printing of the catalogue of the resulting whole; the Grenville Catalogue was amalgamated a little later, so that not all of it is in the published General Catalogue. This began to appear in 1881, and in 1905 a supplement bringing it up to 1900 completed it. You probably all know it, but I have often found that it is possible to use a catalogue for years without understanding its scheme. There are one or two points which may help you in your future use of this enormous and complex work.

Anonyma are the bane of catalogues. There are several ways of dealing with them. One is the detestable habit of simply entering them under the name of the author, real or supposed. Others are to take the heading from the first word, or the first noun, or a "key-word" (about the choice of which cataloguers may lavish all the golden day in metaphysical argument), or a person or place occurring in the title, if it be the subject of the book. The Museum plan is to choose any proper noun or adjective (and in earlier days "Protestant" was considered to be one), and failing that the first noun. This was probably a half-hearted attempt to get round the absence of a subject catalogue. In practice it is a curse; and it is well that readers should understand it.

The second point concerns arrangement. The known author of any anonymous book has a cross-reference to each anonymous edition of it. Thus Swift has a cross-reference for each edition of *Tale of a Tub* to TALE, the (correct) heading. But in a minor heading, which has not been neatly subdivided by the various works, these cross-references are mixed with any other cross-references, such as those to headings of series, to biographers, etc., in one alphabetical order of the heading referred to. This frightful system, which results in chaos, was abolished (but, alas, it could not be retrospectively abolished) by Arthur Miller, while the printing of the catalogue was in mid-career. He devised what we call the main-title cross-reference, in which the title of the book precedes the reference, and governs the alphabetical arrangement of the entry—thus bringing together where they should be, in one chronological order, all editions of the same book.[1] References for books published under initials in the unreformed parts of the catalogue (the beginning and end of the alphabet) are still in the even curter form of a mere single reference of form from the author's name to the initials, very easy to overlook, with no separate entries for separate editions, nor even any mention of the title of the work;[2] and throughout the catalogue pseudonyms are still so treated; with rare exceptions; of these Richard Brathwaite, who wrote under some fifteen ingenious pseudonyms, and whose heading began accordingly with

[1] *E.g.* SWIFT (Jonathan) *Dean of St Patrick's.* The Journal of a Modern Lady....By the Author of Cadenus and Vanessa. Pp. 23. 1729. 8°. *See* JOURNAL.

[2] *E.g.* DELONEY (Thomas). *See* D., T.

27

a bewildering string of uninformative cross-refer-ences,[1] is an extreme instance.

In the sets kept at the Museum itself the pub-lished catalogue is laid down in large album volumes, and the accessions are cut up from the parts published monthly and incorporated as far as may be opposite what would be their places in "column". But sometimes they are crowded over a leaf, and both "column" and "accessions" should be examined.

I will not instruct you in the nature of the cata-logue of the Library of our own University. My own opportunities of using it have been lamentably few. It is of course in print, from 1886 with the aid of the *Bulletin*, but not published as a whole, and to consult it means a visit to Cambridge; this is a draw-back to which there are compensations other than bibliographical, at any rate for a Cambridge man.

The publication of general catalogues, the mass of which must of necessity duplicate that of the Museum, has become too great a financial burden on University Libraries which have to house the national output of books. An industrious compiler

---

[1] *E.g.* BRATHWAIT (Richard). *See* MULTIBIBUS, alias DRINKMUCH (Blasius), *pseud.* [*Jus potandi.*]
— — *See* NEPENTHIACUS (Eucapnus) *Neapolitanus, pseud.* [*Smoking Age.*]
The insertion of the bracketed titles is the reform which has made these cross-references serviceable.

of library statistics, Dr Enrique Sparn, of Cordoba, Argentine, has recently shewn (*El Crecimiento de las Grandes Bibliotecas de la Tierra durante el primer cuarto de siglo XX. I. Las Bibliotecas Universitarias con mas de 100,000 volumenes*. Academia nacional de ciencias, miscelanea No. 13. Cordoba, 1926) that on the average the libraries of the greater European Universities have doubled, while those of North America have trebled, in the last quarter of a century. It is therefore not unnatural that the latest general catalogues of the other libraries of deposit and research are all older than that of the Museum.

The Bodleian's last published catalogue dates from 1843–51, and it does not include one of the two great accessions to its English stores which came in the first half of the nineteenth century, the Douce collection. Thereafter it was kept up to date with manuscript slips, but printing has been resumed in recent years.

The catalogues of some other great libraries must be reckoned with; those of the Advocates' Library, now happily become the Scottish National Library, published in 1867–79; and that of Trinity College, Dublin, to which I fear recent changes have brought less hope, published in 1864–87. It is only natural that these should supplement English libraries chiefly in books printed in Scotland and Ireland, and that for instance we should turn to Trinity College, Dublin, for all those piracies of

29

the eighteenth century, and for obscure editions of Swift, of Sheridan and other Anglo-Irish authors (how Swift would have disliked to hear himself so called!); but in no class are they to be neglected.

The next of these catalogues, that of the John Rylands Library, Manchester, is much smaller than the others, dating as it does from the beginnings of the foundation, in 1899. But its three quarto volumes have the great advantage of having been edited by Edward Gordon Duff, who had not then given up stationary librarianship for peripatetic bibliographical research. A considerably larger catalogue is the latest in date of the class, that of Edinburgh University, which was published in three large volumes in 1918–23. The Library is notably rich in early Scottish books, but it is also important among general collections.

BOOKSELLERS' AND COLLECTORS' GUIDES

Also general in scope, and therefore appropriately regarded as supplementary to the large library catalogues, are guides for book-collectors and booksellers. English book-collectors, and with them English bibliographers, are much less handsomely provided with these than are their French counterparts. Against Brunet, Le Petit, Rahir, Vicaire, and others we have only two books.

The earlier and more copious, but less trustworthy, of these is the celebrated *Bibliographer's
Manual of English Literature* by William Thomas
Lowndes, originally published in 1834, and probably inspired by the success of Brunet's *Manuel du
Libraire*, which had in a score of years gone
through three editions; but with this difference,
that Brunet is (for a Frenchman) international,
while Lowndes is strictly national in his scope.
His records of prices, of course, like those in Brunet,
are now derisory; no doubt at the time they served
their turn. He is very uneven, and without being
checked from other sources his statements cannot
be accepted. He fell into poverty, and from in-
dependent bookselling came to cataloguing for
the prosperous Henry George Bohn, the publisher
of the cheap series. Bohn took over his book, and
in 1857–64 re-edited and greatly enlarged it, but
without much improving its character for accuracy.
Yet in the more important headings he is fairly
full and trustworthy, and there was no other work
of the kind then in existence. Dipping into
Lowndes I find that of the eighteen (or possibly
more) editions of *Pilgrim's Progress*, pt 1, printed
before 1700, he gives fifteen; and that of the editions of Sidney's *Arcadia* printed up to 1725 he
omits only three. I had not expected anything like
so good a show. Three years after the completion
of Bohn's edition Hazlitt (of whom more in due

course) attacked it in the preface to his *Handbook* with a savage contempt from which modesty and a sense of his own frequent lapses should have kept him.

Quite recently a similar manual, aimed at the same public, has been produced by Mr Seymour de Ricci. His *Book Collector's Guide*, N.Y., 1921, is in its scope much more restricted than Lowndes, since it is in fact confined to the well-known names in English literature. The record of recent prices paid for copies is, of course, a feature which is of purely ephemeral interest, for these prices will before long be as irrelevant as those in Lowndes and Brunet. But on the other hand its author's remarkable knowledge of the pedigrees and location of copies finds play, and this and the distinctions of issues, etc., belong to the newer school of bibliography. Where only a handful of copies is known, he gives the present location of them all. And the existence of a respectable bibliography is always noted.

BOOK-TRADE LISTS OF CURRENT BOOKS

From the mid-sixteenth century the book-trade has itself, though for quite unliterary and un-bibliographical motives, kept a record of current publication, imperfect, indeed, and only partly accessible in print, but of great value. In 1556 the Crown incorporated the Company of Stationers, and presently gave it the monopoly, except for the two Universities, of printing. This, of course, was designed to control, through the Company, the production of undesirable literature, the only kind of literature in which statesmen, as such, are interested. All new publications were to be licensed by the Bishop of London, in whose diocese the Company was, and registered under the hands of the Wardens. This celebrated Register records not merely the new books, but transfers of copy-rights and all the ordinary records of the careers of the members of a City Company, from which much collateral information can be got. Fees of 6*d*. for a book and 4*d*. for a ballad were paid; and the amount of the fee is often our only indication as to which class an entry belongs to. The clerks employed were among the least careful of their race, and they appear (at least sometimes) to have taken down titles read aloud; all which does not assist identification of the books.

It might be supposed that the Bishop's licensing chaplains would have kept for reference the copies licensed. But either books were licensed in manu-script, or this precaution was neglected; certainly there is no trace of any official store of these copies having ever existed. Yet unless the licensed copy, whether manuscript or proof, were preserved, it is difficult to see what was to prevent a printer from inserting offensive matter after licensing and before publishing. Entering at Stationers' Hall was never universally practised; not only risky books, but also many ordinary ones, were issued without license, and apparently with impunity. In our time entry at Stationers' Hall was often either a preliminary to a lawsuit or the mark of an amateur publisher. The Copyright Act of 1911 omitted all mention of it. But a Register like the Stationers', entry in which, while voluntary, should be legal evidence, is an undoubted need.

From 19 July 1557 to 1640, with a regrettable gap from 1570 to 1576, which occurs in the original, the Registers were transcribed and published by Edward Arber in 1875–94. For the years from 1641 to 1708 this was followed in 1914 by a transcript made by Mr Henry Plomer for Mr Briscoe Eyre, and presented by him to the Roxburghe Club. Both these sets were unfortunately produced in small numbers and are too expensive for the humble working bookman, who must seek them in large libraries. Also neither has an index of books.

From this point on the printed Register fails us. The first Copyright Act, that of 1709 [8 Anne c. 19], followed on the lapsing in 1695 of the Licensing Act of 1662. The necessity for the Company's

Register of new books therefore largely disappeared. The later Registers remain in manuscript at Stationers' Hall.

Unofficial trade lists of current books began early. In 1618 William Jaggard, whose subterranean activities in piratically reprinting quarto plays of Shakespeare formed the matter of a brilliant series of lectures given on this foundation, printed a catalogue of books then in the press; and in the next half-century appeared various small lists. From 1617 to 1628 the Royal Printers, Bonham Norton and John Bill, published a London edition of the Frankfurt Fair *Messkatalog*, under the title *Catalogus Universalis pro nundinis Francofurtensibus*; the numbers of this from 1622 to 1626 have a supplement of English books, since, as is natural, there was no great demand at a cosmopolitan fair for vernacular books, and it must be confessed that England did not contribute very largely to the common European stock of learned literature. Another of these minor private lists worth mentioning is William London's *Catalogue of the most vendible books* (with supplements, 1657–60). For these and the rest there is full information to be had in Adolf Growoll's *Three Centuries of English Book-Trade Bibliography* (Dibdin Club, N.Y., 1903) and the list of these sources appended to it by Wilberforce Eames.

A much more important list to us is that

founded in 1668 by the booksellers Starkey and
Clavell, under the title of *Mercurius Librarius*. It
died in 1711, and for the last two years or so only
a single number survives. The original numbers
are very rare. They were transcribed and published as the *Term Catalogues* by Arber. Possibly
in consequence of having underprinted his *Transcript of the Stationers' Register*, Arber overprinted
the *Term Catalogues*; the three large volumes can
be had for about £1, and should be in every
library. The lists appeared four times a year and
are dated by the law terms; they are classified
after a fashion, reprints appearing separately. It
is worth remembering that in the broad classifica-
tion of the *Term Catalogues*, "histories" cover both
actual history and biography, and also fiction. At
this period the line between little biographies and
novelettes is so faint that when I was compiling
my *List of English ·Tales and Romances before 1740*,
I was often compelled to decide for inclusion
or exclusion by testing the conversational, and
especially the amatory, scenes, and treating as
fiction those in which they were written with
circumstance. Unlike the *Stationers' Register*, the
Term Catalogues have indices, but their use is not
recommended to anyone who would continue to
think kindly of their compiler.

The titles appear to have been copied in full
from printed title-pages; sizes and publishers are

given. At first, as might be expected, the new venture was not universally supported. In 1670 about 200 books are announced. But in 1680 this has swollen to nearly 700. It is, of course, probable that in the earlier year the publishing trade had not yet recovered from the Fire of four years before. In that year the *Stationers' Register* records only about 75 licenses, so that Starkey and Clavell deserve our gratitude.

We now come to a long blank, and then there begins the series which, as *The English Catalogue*, is still current, with *The London Catalogue of Books since the year 1700*, issued in 1773. This is practically useless. For the three-quarters of a century it records about 7500 works or an average of 100 books a year—a tenth of the average of what the Museum alone possesses for the previous sixty years. Not that any dates are given, or publishers, or even always authors. Pope, one would say, would at least bulk largely. He is given eight entries, and that figure is made by alternative sizes of editions of his works and Homer. "Dramatic works" run to about fifty entries; only two or three separate editions of single plays are recorded. From this darkness it was that Watt delivered the readers of his generation. Supplements followed, and new collected editions in 1776 (as the *General Catalogue*), 1791 (by W. Bent), 1811 and 1814, and then by volumes for 1800–27, 1810–31 and so on. In 1835

37

a rival *British Catalogue* began, and in 1864 Sampson Low amalgamated them into the *English Catalogue*. The standard had meantime been rising, and dates and publishers were given; the total absence of anything but a short title renders the best of the late eighteenth century lists almost useless. In 1914 the first 35 years of the nineteenth century, hitherto ill served by the *London Catalogue*, were covered by a special retrospective volume of the *English Catalogue*, compiled by Messrs Peddie and Waddington.

The *English Catalogue* has a newborn rival in *Whitaker's Cumulative Booklist*, published quarterly and cumulated in an annual. This is classified, whereas the *English Catalogue* is by author and title; but we need not concern ourselves with it. Nor is there any bibliographical value in another bookseller's tool issued by the same firm (Whitaker, of the *Almanack*), *The Reference Catalogue of Current Literature*, issued every three or four years, which simply consists of the chief publishers' newest lists bound together, and provided with a terribly inadequate index. It is therefore just a list of most of the books in print at any one time and no more. You can, if it be worth doing, learn from it pretty nearly when any particular book went out of print. Provincial and technical books do not always appear in these lists; their publishers have other means of reaching their publics.

I have brought these notes down to our own day for the sake of finishing the story, and because literature is after all still going on. But I take it that our special interest is in that of earlier centuries, where the reputations are settled and the influence of fashion, and of fashion's child, that pathetic person the speculator in modern first editions, is less than that of solid criticism. Let us go back to the other bibliographical sources for the different periods, beginning with the introduction of printing.

Interest in the earliest English printing began early. Pepys had some; his books to 1558, mostly English, have been catalogued by Gordon Duff as part III of the still incomplete catalogue of the Library. Though Burton was before Pepys in perceiving the interest of vernacular popular literature, his attitude was clearly not historical, for all the books bequeathed by him to the Bodleian and Christ Church are of his own time, as may be seen in the catalogue by Mr Strickland Gibson and Mr Needham which appears in the third part of the Oxford Bibliographical Society's *Proceedings*. The early and mid-eighteenth century was the time of the first serious work on early English books as such.

This was the time when Harley's great English

library was being collected; while Bagford, the assiduous collector of title-pages and fragments, and Joseph Ames, the original author of the *Typographical Antiquities*, 1749, were at work. Bagford's collections were bought by Harley, and passed among his manuscripts to the British Museum. They have never been indexed; the title-pages at least could and should be. But the whole study was put on a new basis by the great work of William Herbert. Herbert had acquired Ames's book and materials, and in 1785–90 he brought out his new and vastly enlarged and improved edition of it, based on personal examination of all the books he could see—and he had a fine library at Cheshunt,—on researches in the manuscript Stationers' Registers, and on infinite correspondence with like-minded men.

His book is conceived from the typographical rather than from the literary side. English printers from Caxton to 1600 are arranged chronologically; a memoir is given to each, and is followed by a list of the productions of his press, pretty fully described. After Westminster and London printers follow those of the provinces, then Scotland and Ireland, then printers of English books printed overseas, and ἀδέσποτα. It is difficult to praise Herbert too highly. Many of the books he recorded have since vanished again, and he is our only evidence for them. Would that all bibliographical evidence for the existence of lost books were as good!

From 1810 to 1819 Thomas Frognall Dibdin, the grandiose author of the *Bibliographical Decameron* and the *Bibliomania*, Lord Spencer's librarian at Althorp, published the first four volumes of a projected revision and enlargement of Herbert's Ames. There is of course new matter in it, and it is well illustrated—those were the palmy days of fine book production in England—but Dibdin is neither very accurate nor at all concise, and Herbert's own edition is still the standard. In 1899 the Bibliographical Society issued from the single surviving copy in Sion College Library an old index, of unknown origin, to the pair, a serious lack in both, and so made them more usable by the literary as well as by the typographical student.

This was the period of that energetic literary antiquary, Sir Samuel Egerton Brydges, whose series of bibliographical magazines, consisting of accounts of and extracts from rare old editions, is still a useful hunting ground. They are *Censura Literaria*, 10 vols., 1805–9, *The British Bibliographer* (with Joseph Haslewood), 4 vols., 1810–14, and *Restituta*, 4 vols., 1814–16.

But in 1861–3 *The Life and Typography of William Caxton*, by William Blades the printer, whose collections are housed as his memorial at St Brides, brought the study of the origin of English printing

41

a long step further. The abridged later editions embody fresh knowledge. Proctor's *Index* of the early printed books in the Museum and Bodleian in 1898 (the date of vol. II) gave, I believe for the first time, a scientifically arranged conspectus of the work of the few English presses for the quarter of a century before 1500; but with the necessary limitation that not nearly all the books are to be found in these two libraries. Gordon Duff wrote in 1905, for the Caxton Club of Chicago, a brief but very clear and well-illustrated account of Caxton, correcting Blades in many places, notably in giving the true explanation of Wynkyn de Worde's celebrated lines about Caxton printing Bartholomaeus at Cologne, corroboration of which has lately been found among the Cologne Archives by Lt.-Col. J. G. Birch—one result of the Allied occupation of the Rhine in which both sides may take pleasure. And in 1909 Mr Seymour de Ricci carried our knowledge a step further by publishing (as the Bibliographical Society's Monograph xv) a census of all known copies of all Caxtons, a work which is a mine of knowledge about the migrations of copies and the libraries of the English book-collectors who have gathered and recorded early English books; its value in this way reaches much beyond Caxton.

Duff's collections were edited at last by him, with the help of Dr Henry Thomas, for the Bibliographical Society in 1917, as *Fifteenth Century*

English Books. The Government had (owing to the personal interest of Mr Asquith, and doubtless at a favourable moment when the attention of economical statesmen was directed elsewhere) awakened to the existence of bibliography, and aided the publication by a grant of £100. Some ten years before this event Hazlitt (in the preface of his last volume, 1903) had written the following bitter words: "I cannot afford to spend any more money in printing my labours, and as I live in England and not in Germany or Russia, it is useless to expect help from the Government."

Fifteenth Century English Books is an exhaustive series of standard descriptions under authors or titles, followed by facsimiles and a short-title list in "Proctor-order". It is as final as any bibliography can well be—which is not saying much, when your subject-matter keeps growing, that being indeed part of the pleasure of the sport. It records 431 books, two-thirds at least of which are in the English language in whole or in part, except the small academic output of the Oxford press, only one book from which, a Latin grammar, contains any vernacular. Nearly half the books are known from unique copies or from fragments, and during the twenty odd years of Mr Duff's searching he states that no less than fifty-four new books or sheets came to light. By the evidence of surviving twin volumes, or of scattered woodcuts appearing later and evidently cut for a single book, several

43

are inferred but not known. One of these is *Reynard the Fox*; and I cannot help thinking that if no copy of Reynard, only one apiece of so many, and only two of Aesop and Malory, have survived, there may well have been a Mandeville too, and that Wynkyn de Worde's edition of 1496 may have been, like so many of his larger books, merely a reprint, to meet an assured demand, of an edition first printed by his more adventurous master.

The next half-century, that up to the incorporation of the Stationers' Company, is not yet so well covered. But in the early years of this century the Bibliographical Society published a series of handlists of London printers and their productions, which have proved most useful by recording the changes of addresses, devices, etc., to date undated books, but which are rather tiresome to the literary student, since no author or title index was added, and one can hardly guess, if one does not know, whether it was Pynson or de Worde, Copland or Grafton, who printed a piece. Gordon Duff had a large hand in these, and to him is very much due the number of out-of-the-way libraries from which copies are recorded, with the result that the Museum, Oxford and Cambridge, where one expects to find a high percentage, are shewn to have a very low one. The literature of this period, in fact, while of extraordinary interest (since it is at the turn of the tide to modern forms of the

44

language and of verse), is buried in small books nearly always as rare as Caxton's folios, and much more elusive, in libraries scattered over Great Britain and the United States.

Duff gathered his knowledge of the typography of this period into his two series of Sandars lectures, in 1904 and 1911 (published in 1906 and 1912), covering respectively the London and the provincial printers; the latter contains a handlist of the books from all the country presses, which supplements the lists for London published by the Society, and of course goes much beyond Herbert's. Andrew Maunsell's catalogue of English books known to him in 1595 I have already spoken of.

Early is a relative term at any time; and not least when applied to printing. Some older special catalogues, including S. R. Maitland's of Lambeth (1845), Collett's of Caius (1850), and Sinker's of Trinity (1885), take 1600 as their terminal mark. Joseph Ritson, in his *Bibliographia Poetica*, 1802, had confined himself to the English poets of the fifteenth and sixteenth centuries. But most, following Arber's *Transcript of the Stationers' Register*, 1875, and the Museum Catalogue of 1884, go to 1640, the date after which the theatre closed and the Civil War produced the embattled scribblers who are the normal product of such times. With few exceptions 1640 is the limit of date set to John Payne Collier's very valuable *Biblio-*

45

*graphical and Critical Account of the rarest books in the
English Language*, 2 vols., 1865, in which he incorporated the matter of his earlier *Bridgewater
Catalogue*, describing a large number of rare early
books with full bibliographical and literary notes,
in the manner of Sir Egerton Brydges. Collier's
work appeared immediately after Bohn's revision
of Lowndes, and immediately before Hazlitt's
Handbook, and the three books may be regarded
as the link between the old bibliography and the
new. In the last generation a very considerable
number of special catalogues of English books to
1640 have appeared; indeed few libraries of any
note can have failed to produce one. The Museum's
catalogue of 1884 is not a very creditable performance; the titles were picked out from the mass that
were then going to press for the *General Catalogue*;
imprints were expanded, and two indices, a very bad
one of printers, and a very good one of classes and
titles, were added. This latter index is the only one
of its kind for the period anywhere, so far as I know
It is a great thing to be able to look up Herbals or
Ballads and find a list, or, if you have a copy without
a title-page, to be able to look up the running title
with a good chance of finding the author. It should
be remembered that since the publication of this
catalogue in 1884 very large additions have been
made to the library for the period, as books before
1640 have been methodically collected.

One of Duff's first proceedings as Librarian of the John Rylands Library was to follow the Museum with a catalogue of the English books to 1640 in the new library; this, which was published in 1895, is valuable as containing entries, both more brief and more accurate than Dibdin's, of this part of the Althorp Library.

A much more carefully thought-out scheme is that of the corresponding catalogue for our University Library, conceived by Dr Jenkinson and Mr Sayle and worked out by the latter (1904–7). Here we have the typographical method, the idea of Bradshaw, which had then recently been applied so notably to the Museum's incunabula that it is generally called "Proctor-order", adapted to English books. Light, where the order of the alphabet leaves darkness, was promptly shed on many presses, not least on those Continental presses printing the English books which neither the *Stationers' Register* nor Maunsell would record. The student who merely wishes to find the works of an author is of course provided with indices to that and other matters.[1] The Bibliographical Society followed with the early

[1] There is, by the way, in this catalogue an ingenious printer's "sort" which I have never seen anywhere else, and which I recommend. It is the *broken* square bracket [ ] to represent words supplied in a title on account of imperfection in the copy described, the complete square bracket being employed for other supplied words, as usual.

47

books in Narcissus Marsh's Library, Dublin, and then those at Emmanuel, and there have been many other smaller lists. The Bodleian has never produced a special catalogue of this scope, a serious gap in the English bibliographer's armour.

But this omission, and that of an author index to the *Hand Lists of London Printers of 1501–56*, were perhaps due to the faith that some day a collective one-line finding-list for all discoverable books to 1640 would be possible; and in fact this was always in the minds of the Bibliographical Society's Council. The work has been taken in hand; first by Mr Redgrave, with Mr Barwick, on the latter's retirement from the Keepership of Printed Books, then by Mr Pollard, also retiring in his turn. The result is now (1927) published. The catalogue contains about 26,000 titles. Short as the titles are, enough is given to distinguish editions and issues; and much care has been taken to separate or identify authors or books of similar names or titles. A good case of the latter is to be seen in the various rival collections, taken originally in shorthand and sent to different publishers, of the popular sermons of "silver-tongued Smith". Locations of several copies are given, where possible at least one on either side of the Atlantic, which ocean is clearly (if inadequately) represented by a semi-colon. The catalogue should be a great saving of trouble; but the fuller catalogues, and especially those arranged typographically, will still not be superseded; and there will be room for much detailed work, especially on the books printed overseas.

After 1640 we have the exiguous help of the *Stationers' Register*, and beside it for the next twenty years the great collection of contemporary literature made by George Thomason. Thomason's intelligence in perceiving that the fugitive literature of a troubled time would have permanent value met with no reward in his lifetime. It was only when George III came to the throne, a century later, that the books came to be public property, for the price, very low then and absurd now, of £300; nor do they seem to have attracted much attention till Carlyle, in his full and heightened style, greatly preferred them to "all the sheepskins in the Tower and other places, for informing the English what the English were in former times". From that date they have been, as they deserve to be, one of the chief sources, literary as well as historical, for the period.

Thomason excluded from his collection everything (except single sheets) in folio; but with that limitation he was omnivorous. The 22,000 pieces include poetry, medicine, and indeed every sort of writing. We owe to him our copy of Milton's *Tractate of Education*, of which only five copies survive, and many unique pieces. He did not get much provincially printed matter, as indeed might be expected, and as Mr Madan's *Oxford Books* clearly shews. What proportion to the London output his books represent is doubtful, but it is so high as to make it curious that it is not higher. There is at present nothing adequate to check it by. The Museum has trusted too much to the possession of the Thomason Tracts, and has bought comparatively little of the period. The average per year, about 1000, is pretty much that of the English book in the Museum for 1641–1700; and when the Museum's short-title catalogue for those 60 years is out I should expect to find another 20 per cent. at least of Civil War and Commonwealth books.

As soon as the burden of producing the *General Catalogue* was lifted, the Trustees turned to special catalogues, and, with the fifteenth century books, the Thomason Tracts received the earliest attention. In the plan of this catalogue, which appeared in two volumes in 1908, the historian is better served than the literary student or the bibliographer; and this doubtless represents the predilections of George Fortescue, who as Keeper had control of and a large personal share in editing it, though the mass of the work was done by Mr Sharp and Mr Marsden. Thomason, methodical man, had the habit (not quite consistent) of writing at the foot of the title-page the exact date, probably that on which he received the copy, but also nearly enough, we may be sure, that of publication. This enabled Fortescue to produce a catalogue in a chronological arrangement, in which, as in a modern newspaper, we can follow the ebb and flow of rumour and opinion in London from day to day. The tracts unprovided with these exact dates, but dated or datable to the year, follow at the year's end. Newspapers, the infancy of which in this period is largely known to us from this collection, are separately catalogued at the end. The index is large, but is conceived on historical lines. Many tracts are not separately indexed, but are merged in large subject headings like PARLIAMENT or CHARLES I, and it is very common for booksellers in their catalogues to assert that Civil War and Commonwealth pamphlets are not in the Thomason catalogue, when in fact they are. What deceives booksellers (though no doubt they are not too unwilling to be deceived in this way) may also, I suppose, sometimes deceive students of literature; so that I may be pardoned for mentioning a small point.

The undoubted value of the chronological order adopted in this catalogue makes one wonder why it has been tried for no other period, at least for the literature dealing simply with current public affairs. Would not a similar list for the pamphlets of the Popish Plot time be just as instructive?

And if we carry our minds back, why not for the pre-Thomason period? The bulk of actual contemporary printed criticism on events before the Civil War is comparatively small; under the Tudors and early Stuarts the political journalist or his ancestor had to walk warily, witness the fates of Stubbes and of Prynne, Burton and Bastwick.

Of Restoration literature there is no special bibliography. The *Term Catalogues* and *Stationers' Register* help; and there is one large series which covers the whole period from 1474 to 1700. This is Hazlitt's. In 1867, soon after the appearance and success of Bohn's Lowndes, William Carew Hazlitt published his *Handbook of the popular, poetical and dramatic literature of Great Britain from the Invention of printing to the Restoration*; and in 1876, 1882, 1889, 1892 and 1903 he followed it up with series of *Collections and Notes* or *Bibliographical Collections and Notes*, and Supplements, in which the *terminus ante quem* is advanced from 1660 to 1700. Each volume likewise has a supplement of titles accumulated while the body of the volume was in the press. To the maddening labour of satisfying oneself that a book was not recorded by Hazlitt, rather than to his considerable inaccuracy (said to be due to noting books hurriedly on the backs of envelopes), is perhaps to be attributed the sub-acid flavour noticeable in the tone in which bibliographers speak of him. That is, of the pre-Gray era. In 1893 G. J. Gray made Hazlitt usable by indexing the parts up to 1889. This index is indeed very far from thorough accuracy; but without it Hazlitt's *Collections* are a morass. One thing, however, we do owe to Hazlitt. He was the first bibliographer after Herbert to give a collation by quires in any but a long analytical description of a book, and he gives them habitually. It is so easy a thing to give for all but the longest books that it ought always to be given. Again, the practice of prefixing an engraved frontispiece (generally a portrait of the author) to a book was perhaps more general in the seventeenth century than it has ever been before or since. These portraits have been in most copies removed by unscrupulous petty dealers and sold separately, and, as there is generally no mention of them in the book and the plate leaf forms no part of a text-sheet, there is nothing to shew that anything is missing. At that time the Museum Library, in the enjoyment of its increased grant for purchase (long ago reduced again), combined with low prices, was getting in books by the hundred with what Mr Pollard has described as "faith-inspired general buying". The faith that almost any book would probably fill some gap and be of use was justified. Not so the faith that all the books were perfect; and without a handy guide like Hazlitt's, or in its absence without long and probably fruitless research for which time could not be spared, there was no protection against buying copies robbed of their portraits or imperfect in other subtle ways, and in consequence the Museum has too many of them.

When Hazlitt died in 1913 he bequeathed his bibliographical accumulations to the Museum, and (after a life interest which is still in existence) a sum of money, with the charge of bringing out a consolidated edition of his *Handbook* and *Collections*. Unfortunately, by the time that that can appear we shall have the *Short Title Catalogue of Books to 1640*, and the Museum's *Short Title Catalogue from 1641 to 1700*, as well as the *Thomason Catalogue*, and other catalogues elsewhere, so that much of the consolidated Hazlitt, when it does appear, will simply duplicate easily accessible information. The rest, being the larger part, of the money bequest is to be used for acquiring for the Museum early English books.

The Grolier Club, of New York, has done more justice to individual rare books than Hazlitt could on the scale he had chosen, in its two very finely produced and illustrated volumes: *A Catalogue of original and early Editions of...English Writers from Langland to Wither* (and *from Wither to Prior*), 1893, 1905, in which most of the title-pages are reproduced and full collations given.

With the eighteenth century we come to a quite

different state of things. The collectors, until recently, paid small attention to it, and what attention they paid was to the original editions of the great books. The National Library had led the way in doing nothing in particular in the matter. It was generally, but tacitly, supposed that the accession of the King's Library, formed during the century, backed by copyright deposit for its latter years, had provided the Museum with all it could want. A sufficient commentary on that supposition is to be found in the fact that the Museum does not possess copies of the first publications of Gay or Collins, or of the first editions of Watts's or the Wesleys' Hymns, and that it has just acquired the first editions of Smart's *Song to David* and of *Tristram Shandy*.

In the last two years the Bodleian has been issuing in its *Quarterly Record* systematic lists of its desiderata, mostly in eighteenth and early nineteenth century English books, and with very promising results.

Not only have the greatest public and private libraries not methodically collected the eighteenth century; there are no general bibliographies for it. The *Term Catalogues* cease; the *Stationers' Register* fails us, until someone prints some more of it. Of the *London Catalogue* of books printed between 1700 and 1773 I have already given you my opinion. Watt is really our chief bibliographical source.

55

But there is another side to the picture. We are now reaching a time of whose social, and consequently whose literary life we have many records, a time from which we have countless memoirs and letters. For every man or woman of the seventeenth century whom we feel we know—people such as Pepys, Walton, Dorothy Osborne—there are twenty in the next century. They are our familiars; and familiarity breeds bibliography. Practically every really big man, and here and there a small man, of letters of the century has found his bibliographer. Moreover, Nichols's *Literary Anecdotes* and *Illustrations* form such an immense repertory of the literary history of the period, and from such original sources, that though not in bibliographical form they can hardly be left quite unmentioned.

Two other sources present themselves. The practice of using the blank last leaf or leaves of a book to advertise the publisher's other productions had grown up in the latter half of the seventeenth century, and is found in full vogue in the eighteenth; its modern descendant is the detachable section on thin paper bearing the publisher's list of new or cognate books, which differs in being no part of the book itself. There is one warning I would offer, based on experience bought by my own errors. It is not safe to assume that an entry in one of these lists implies that an edition bearing that publisher's name ever existed. If you read

The Life and Errors of John Dunton (a work full not
only of solid information but of the most delightful
absurdities), you will find that it was the practice
of booksellers to exchange parts of editions with
each other. It is clear that many entries in publishers' lists represent such copies, sufficiently
numerous to be worth advertising, taken over by
exchange from another publisher. In my *List of
English Tales and Romances*, not realising this, I fear
that I swelled the roll-call with ghosts, and others
have probably done the same. After Dunton's
time the sharing of an edition was arranged before
publication, and the names of all the shareholding
publishers were habitually given in the imprint of
all copies.

There are also the advertisements of new books
in the newspapers and later in the literary magazines, notably the *Gentleman's Magazine*. The
editors and bibliographers of Defoe, Swift and
Pope have to look to the newspapers of the day at
every turn, and this must be true of other and
lesser pamphleteers. One of the numerous tasks
that still await courageous workers is to go through
and index all the book announcements in the newspapers, say from 1700 up to the foundation of
the *Gentleman's Magazine* in 1731. Luckily Charles
Burney, whose collection of old newspapers in the
Museum is the largest anywhere, had them bound
up (rather after the manner of Thomason), not

by set but by date. Thus all the papers of one week are together.

The nineteenth century is too vast for any collective period bibliography. The trade lists were improving; and the Copyright Acts were revised and enforced in and from 1842, so that in the libraries of deposit a really large proportion of the output can be found. Watt covers some of the previous third of the century; and there is the retrospective list by Messrs Peddie and Waddington of the London and other Catalogues for 1801–35, to run with the *English Catalogue* and complete the century. But these, valuable as they are, still leave the period bibliographically rather dark, though not in the inspissated obscurity of the preceding age.

When we turn from large general repertories of the books produced in the successive periods, we have to find what support is given, and what gaps filled, by lists of books in special classes. The classes that will be found to have yielded these lists are naturally those which excite interest and affection; where your treasure is, there will your bibliography be also.

We find then that collections and lists have been made of the books produced in particular localities, large and small, by members of particular churches, in particular literary forms, and by particular authors.

Scottish bibliographers have been active for a century and more, in proportion to the rarity, the small bulk and the interest of their material. They may count among their pioneers no less a person than the Laird of Monkbarns, or (to speak more exactly) his great creator. Both Edinburgh and Glasgow have societies, and the libraries of the Advocates (now the National Library), of the four Universities and some others, public and private, such as John Scott's and the Britwell, are or have been rich in Scottish books. The standard book on the early Scottish printers is Dickson and Edmond's *Annals of Scottish Printing from...1507 to the beginning of the seventeenth century*, 1890; and all later work is ultimately a development from their foundation. Edmond also produced the chief study of the Aberdeen press.

This typographical study laid the foundation for a more literary one. In 1904 the Edinburgh Bibliographical Society published *A List of Books printed in Scotland before 1700*, by the late Harry Gidney Aldis, of the University Library. This is probably the best book of its kind in existence. It is not a series of standard descriptions, like Duff's *Fifteenth Century English Books*, or it would be much larger than it is. It is a one-line finding

59

list, the books set out year by year, with the libraries where they are to be found; and followed by notes on the printers and publishers and indices of authors and titles.

This list is modestly described as provisional, the forerunner and, as it were, ground-bait for a full-dress bibliography of the books. The Society has collected a considerable quantity of standard descriptions, and will welcome others, made on the models laid down by Aldis and printed at the beginning of his list, towards this work.

Aldis gives a very good idea of the dispersion of Scottish books. He gives references to eighteen libraries for copies; and his unlocated entries doubtless represent many more. Up to the end of 1600 he gives 341 books and pieces; of these the largest share is in the Advocates' Library, represented in his entries by A, which has 81 or less than one in four. Of the 105 books of 1699, on the other hand, that library has 69, or almost exactly two in three. Unfortunately Aldis, anxious for brevity, never gives more than one location, adopting a sort of scale of precedence, so that it is impossible to say what sort of proportion is to be found anywhere else.[1]

[1] I much regret that without his excuse (nor any but inexperience and the fact that Mr Madan had not then taught us the need of what he calls "degressive bibliography") I did the same in my *Tales and Romances*, so that "B.M." does not mean that a book is not in Bodley or U.L.C., though "U.L.C." does mean that there is none in B.M. or Bodley.

The Edinburgh Bibliographical Society has published other detailed lists and studies, notably those by John Scott of the literature of Mary Queen of Scots, 1896, and of the Darien Company, 1906. Scott died in 1903, and his library, containing much of the subject-matter of these bibliographies, was dispersed.

The rarity of early Scottish books can again be well gauged by a recent publication, the list of books printed at St Andrews before the departure of Raban for Aberdeen in 1622, by the University Librarian, Mr G. H. Bushnell, first issued as part of Professor J. H. Baxter's *Collections towards a Bibliography of St Andrews*, 1926, and subsequently separately, revised. Of the 46 books there registered, no library has more than 14, in the National Library of Scotland; and the British Museum comes next with 10.

For Scottish books later than 1699 there is no general guide but the catalogues of the Advocates' and Edinburgh University Libraries; articles on particular presses, both earlier and later than this date, are numerous; notably Cowan's on the Holyrood Press of 1686–8.

Irish bibliography is obscurer than Scottish. But we have Trinity College, Dublin, with its catalogue, and the very fine Hibernian collection in our own University Library, largely that of Henry Bradshaw, presented part by and part in memory of him. The Bradshaw family came from North Ireland, and some of the collection was made before Henry's time: but he added much to it; and his letter of gift to the Vice-Chancellor, written in 1870, is one of the most self-effacing and beautiful documents of the kind in existence, worthy of its author. The catalogue of this collection, by Sayle, published in 1916, is our best source for finding Irish books. It is arranged under printers, like Sayle's earlier work; in the later period this is perhaps a pity; but an index covers much. The earlier part of it, being the Dublin printed books, may be compared with Mr E. R. McCracken Dix's *Catalogue of Early Dublin-printed Books, 1601 to 1700* (1898–1905). The same industrious bibliographer has produced, in the *Irish Book Lover* and various other Irish literary journals, a quantity of articles on early printing in Irish provincial towns. In 1791 there appeared *A General Catalogue of Books in all Languages Arts and Sciences that have been printed in Ireland and published in Dublin from the year 1700 to the present time*. There is no copy of this in the British Museum, I am sorry to say—though it is the sort of book which is the Museum's natural prey; nor is there in the Bradshaw collection.

Printing in the English provinces up to 1556 is well covered by Gordon Duff's second series of Sandars lectures. But with the incorporation of the Stationers' Company and the monopoly of printing granted to its members, provincial printing disappears, except in Oxford and Cambridge, where new presses started work in 1583 and 1585, after a gap dating from the failure of Siberch in 1522.

Oxford books are handsomely dealt with by Mr Falconer Madan, whose *Early Oxford Press*, published by the Oxford Historical Society in 1895, brought the list as complete as may be from pseudo-1468 to 1640. In 1912 he published a fatter volume, *Oxford Books, 1450–1640, 1641–1650*, in which not only is the production of the Oxford press for the period chronicled, but all books relating to Oxford up to 1650 are entered and annotated. The Oxford books of the Civil War are here for the first time carefully examined and distinguished by their typographical peculiarities from the London editions with the same imprints; for while the Court was at Oxford, the Oxford presses were busy producing Royalist pamphlets, which Londoners (at least Royalist Londoners) were anxious to read; but to which London publishers were not anxious to put their names. What they did was to reprint them exactly, retaining the Oxford imprints, and to circulate the reprints *sub rosa*. I have often thought that had the police in the sixteenth and seventeenth centuries been able to employ a few modern trained bibliographers, their efforts to

63

suppress unlawful printing would have been more successful. They did, it is true, occasionally set a printer to catch a printer, but with less than the success they might have hoped for. The work of distinguishing the true from the false is one which should have been, but was not, undertaken in producing the Thomason catalogue of 1908; fortunately Mr Madan was hard on our heels to do our work for us; out of 191 Oxford imprints of 1642, he finds 58 to be London counterfeits; and other years yield similar figures.

For Cambridge we have the large catalogue by the late Robert Bowes, published by himself in 1894; but this, good as it is, and provided with scholarly notes, is confined to the books actually forming part of the collection in stock. As an appendix Bowes printed a one-line list, by the late University Librarian, of Cambridge books from 1521 to 1650. This has been enlarged and carried down another century by Mr S. C. Roberts, in a list appended to his *History of the Cambridge University Press*, 1921.

In support of Robert Bowes and Mr Roberts we have the late J. W. Clark's bequest to the University Library of his Cambridge collection, catalogued in 1912. The great strength of this is, I think, in fugitive nineteenth century pieces.

It is natural that publishing in the two University towns should be largely learned and in the learned languages. The great sources of knowledge about the authors (outside the actual Registers of their Colleges and Universities) are, for Cambridge, Charles and Thompson Cooper's *Athenae Cantabrigienses*, 1858–61, and the new *Alumni Cantabrigienses* by Mr Venn, which began to appear in 1922; and for Oxford an older and more famous book, the parent of the rest, Anthony à Wood's *Athenae Oxonienses*, originally published in 1691–6 (the author died in 1695), second edition 1721, and enlarged by Philip Bliss in the standard edition of 1813–20. The immense merit of Wood is his nearness to the men whose writings he records; his information is largely based on personal knowledge. These books are not exactly bibliographies, but (like Nichols's *Literary Anecdotes*) they are among the foundations on which bibliography rests.

Other provincial presses were those of York, chronicled for the sixteenth, seventeenth and eighteenth centuries by Robert Davies in 1868; Newcastle by Richard Welsford, in *Archaeologia Aeliana*, 1906; in both these places Royalist printing was carried on in the Civil War, as at Oxford, and the products are ill-represented in the Thomason Collection; since what Thomason received was generally a London reprint.

There were also secret and unlawful presses, such as the wandering press from which came the Martin Marprelate tracts of 1588–90; these have been bibliographically studied by Professor Dover Wilson and Mr William Pierce; and the secret Catholic press at or near Birchley Hall in Lancashire in 1613, the books from which were recently exhibited at Wigan, and described by the Librarian, Mr A. J. Hawkes, who also contributed to *The Library* a paper on the press. There were also the series of tracts produced late in the sixteenth century by the unseemly quarrels of the Jesuits and Seculars. These priests were missionaries *in partibus infidelium* and were incarcerated at Wisbech; like the game cocks who were tied up in one bag but failed to take the view of the groom who put them there, that being all the property of his master they must needs be on the same side, they fell on one another. These tracts were excellently described in 1889 by Thomas Graves Law, then Librarian to the Signet at Edinburgh.

When in 1695 the old licensing law lapsed, the limitation of printing to London lapsed as part of it. Before this provincial booksellers' imprints had been common enough; to take one example, many of Baxter's books, while printed in London, bear also the imprint of his Kidderminster agent, Nevill Simmons. But of provincial printing there had been little. In the early years of the eighteenth century the dispersion began. Printers who were not flourishing or who had some connection with a

county town, and "smouters", or journeymen
who worked casually for other men, moved presses
and types and tried their fortune in the country.
The Life of Thomas Gent by himself, which has only
been partly printed, and the manuscript of which
seems to be lost, gives a lively picture of this time.
Gent was a smouter before he went to York.

Many county bibliographies record the work
of the early local presses, though not always in a
form easy to consult; apart from these the Cheshire
press was separately chronicled by J. H. Cooke in
1904; the Devonshire by J. I. Dredge in 1885–7;
the Derbyshire by Alfred Wallis in 1881; the
Nottinghamshire by S. F. Creswell in 1863; the
Lancashire by Mr A. J. Hawkes in 1925. Moreover, most city and borough libraries have local
collections in which are pieces not to be found in
the great national libraries. Thus the Liverpool
City Library published in 1908 a valuable catalogue of *Liverpool Prints and Documents*, which is
only an example, though an outstanding one, of a
type.

The productions of these travelling presses, the
incunabula of the English provinces, are unfortunately hardly ever of intrinsic value. The
demand was for assize-sermons and quack medicines; among the latter being Daffy's Elixir, with
which a century later Amelia Osborne would not
let her mother poison the baby. This connection

between patent medicines and books has clearly
in it something of the immutable nature of things,
since it survives to-day; but its frequency then
seems to shew that the provincial book-trade was
not very prosperous. A more interesting, though
an even less literary, product of these pioneer
presses was the local newspaper; one or two founded
then, such as the *Northampton Mercury*, 1720, and
the *Gloucester Journal*, are still in existence.

Summary information about the provincial, as
about the London, book-trade is to be found in
the series of dictionaries of printers published by the
Bibliographical Society. Gordon Duff's *Century of the
English Book Trade* takes it to 1556, Dr McKerrow's
Dictionary filled the gap to 1640, Mr Plomer's
volume for 1641–67 having already appeared; a
volume for 1668–1725 is now out; and Mr Plomer
has in hand the next half-century, a half-century
for which Nichols's *Anecdotes* are a solid foundation.

In 1922 there began a very ambitious series,
entitled *English Tracts, Pamphlets and Printed Sheets:
a bibliography*, by J. Harvey Bloom. Unfortunately
the plan (for which I understand Mr Bloom
was not responsible) was imperfectly thought
out. The volumes were to deal with the smaller
printed literature of counties, one by one; but
the connection of many of the authors with the
counties they appear under is accidental. Nor is
the definition of a "tract" very clear; it should

have some relation to current or local matters if it is to have any place in such a bibliography. Plays at least should have been excluded. With all these defects the two volumes (probably all) which have appeared, covering Suffolk, Leicestershire, Staffordshire, Warwickshire and Worcestershire, will probably be found to contain titles not easily traced elsewhere and to repay occasional reference when other sources fail.

The Welsh book-trade represented a move forward into the void by pioneers from Shrewsbury and Chester, in the same period, and its fortunes to the present day have been fully treated in a ponderous book by Mr J. Ifano Jones of Cardiff; the National Library of Wales has as yet only a card catalogue, to be consulted on the spot; but of the Welsh collection in the Cardiff City Library a catalogue by Mr John Ballinger and Mr Jones was published in 1898. But the most important bibliography of Welsh books is W. Rowlands's *Cambrian Bibliography*, 1869. The contact, however, between Welsh publishing and English literature is very tenuous.

BIBLIOGRAPHIES OF LITERARY FORMS

Interest may be focussed on the great classes of literary form, and these too do not lack for bibliographical record.

Poetry is too wide a field to be treated as special, and books dealing with it will be regarded as dealing with literature at large. By far the most popular, the most studied and recorded form in England has been the drama. The bibliographical material for the English drama and stage is so enormous, and so accessible, that I hesitate to touch it in this hasty review. It occupies much the best section of a very unequal recent work, Northup's *Register of Bibliographies of the English Language and Literature* (1925), and runs there to about five hundred entries of bibliographies (excluding single authors), play-lists, and catalogues of public and private libraries. I will therefore only mention a handful of outstanding works.

Sir Edmund Chambers's *Mediaeval Stage* contains incidentally the best lists of manuscript texts and other authorities. The period of print, beginning with the circle of Sir Thomas More, with Medwall and Rastell, down to the closing of the theatres in 1642, has aroused more enthusiasm and curiosity than perhaps any other literary movement in the world's history. There is accordingly a wealth of authority for its remains, which amount to about six hundred plays.

The most permanently valuable source of information is the diary of Philip Henslowe, 1591–1609, preserved at Dulwich College. Henslowe, as manager of theatres, employed many dramatists, and his record of his (very economical) payments to them are a primary authority for the authorship of many plays written in collaboration. The diary was edited in 1845 by John Payne Collier, who, for his wantonness, inserted forged entries. It was re-edited by Dr Greg in 1904–8 in trustworthy form.

The earliest play-list to reckon with is Archer's, appended to *The Old Law*, 1656. It is of small authority, and more interest attaches to that of Francis Kirkman, publisher and bookseller, and the not very reputable continuer of Head's *English Rogue*; this list was issued in 1661, with his edition of an old play, *Tom Tyler and his Wife*.

Printed editions of plays written before the closing of the theatres have been completely recorded, from surviving copies and from these lists, by Dr Greg in *A List of English Plays written before 1643 and printed before 1700*, and in a companion *List of Masques*, published by the Bibliographical Society in 1900 and 1902. Dr Greg has now in preparation a full bibliography based on the short titles in these lists. His chief predecessors were Edward Capell, whose *Notitia Dramatica*, 1783, takes plays up to the Restoration; and F. G. Fleay, whose *Bibliographical Chronicle of the English Drama*, 1559–1642, with an element of the perverse and the fantastic, is still a standard work.

The next play-list after Kirkman's was that of

Gerard Langbaine, published at Oxford in 1691, and based on an earlier attack by him on the habit of the dramatists of pillaging foreign plays and romances for their plots. Theatrical "runs" were so short and consequently the production of plays was so rapid that the unfortunate dramatist had to hunt for plots—exactly as the film-producer of the present day has to. Langbaine's *Account of the English Dramatick Poets* (Oxford, 1691, new edition by Charles Gildon, 1699) is our first and indeed our only contemporary record of the Restoration stage, so far as it appeared in print. The record of performances, drawn from Pepys's Diary and similar sources, belongs to another side of dramatic history and is from the literary point of view secondary, except as establishing the order of writing of an author's plays. The play-lists went on in regular series, with that by W. Mears of 1713, D. E. Baker's *Companion to the Playhouse*, 1764, which reappeared in new editions by Isaac Reed in 1782, and by Jones in 1812; revisions by Halliwell-Phillipps (*A Dictionary of Old English Plays to the close of the Seventeenth Century*, 1860), and by W. C. Hazlitt, *A Manual for the Collector and Amateur of Old English Plays*, 1892. This is a goodly "run" for a book published in 1691.

The chief dramatic collections are (or in some cases have been) those of Edward Capell, bequeathed to Trinity, of which a catalogue was published in 1903 by Dr Greg; Edmond Malone, given to the Bodleian by his brother, Lord Sunderlin, in 1815, a special catalogue being printed in 1836; David Garrick, bequeathed to the Museum after Mrs Garrick's death in 1823; Alexander Dyce, bequeathed to the South Kensington Museum, and specially catalogued in 1875; and J. P. Kemble, subsequently in the Chatsworth Library, then bought by Mr Henry Huntington, who resold duplicates and kept the rest in his foundation at San Gabriel. Sir Edmund Gosse's Restoration plays are worth mentioning, and also his account in the catalogue of his library of his happy experiences in collecting them, and their almost indecent cheapness in the London bookshops of his youth.

The Kemble-Devonshire copies have every leaf separately mounted, which does indeed save the frail leaves in turning over, but destroys evidence of make-up.

Specially important dramatic collections in the United States are Mr Huntington's, just mentioned, the Yale Elizabethan Club's, Mr H. C. Folger's, Mr W. A. White's, Mr Marsden Perry's, now sold, and doubtless others. Mr White published a handlist in 1914 and a catalogue in 1926.

Among collections that have been sold at auction are those of Isaac Reed, sold in 1787; Richard Farmer, Master of Emmanuel and University

Librarian, sold in 1789; George Steevens, sold
in 1800, and Lord Mostyn, sold in 1919. Lord
Mostyn possessed the only known copy of the first
English secular play, Medwall's *Fulgens and Lucres*,
which is now at San Gabriel, and has been reproduced in facsimile at the cost of Mr Huntington.
Most of the greatest private collections of English
books have had a good section of the drama; the
only exception I know is the Britwell Library.

You will have noticed the names of nearly all
the great Shakespearean scholars of that generation—all but one. Johnson had almost no old
plays except the first and second folios of Shakespeare; he depended on Garrick's copies, and
records (rather ungratefully) that he had "not
found the possessors of these rarities very com-
municative of them". But that was because,
while Garrick would let him come to Hampton to
see them, he would not lend them to Johnson,
whose habits with books he knew. It must be
added that many of Garrick's copies at the
Museum look as if they had not always been owned
by true bibliophiles.

Perhaps the greatest single accumulation of
records of the English drama is a book which is
not in form a bibliography; the Rev. John
Genest's *Some Account of the English Stage, from the
Restoration in 1660 to 1830* (Bath, 1832), which
occupies ten substantial volumes, requiring pa-

tience and experience to extract the marrow from, and not at all adapted to ready reference. Not to put too fine a point on it, Genest's work is a vast and almost trackless jungle of material, unindexed, and with the minimum of plan. Consult him, use him, as all later workers on the drama have used him, for he has a high reputation for accuracy; but do not try to turn to anything in him quickly or light-heartedly; approach him reverently and with an hour or two to spare.

He was continued to near the end of the nineteenth century by C. W. Scott, in *The Drama of Yesterday and To-day*, 1899.

Two recent books include play-lists for 1660 to 1750; these are Professor Allardyce Nicoll's *History of Restoration Drama*, 1923, and *History of Early Eighteenth Century Drama*, 1925.

One can hardly turn from the drama with no mention of Shakespeare. There are, of course, countless select lists; it will be enough to mention those by Sir Sidney Lee and Sir Edmund Chambers (English Association Pamphlet, no. 60), and by Mr H. Sellers (in the *Library Association Record*, new ser. vol. I, nos. 2–3), and the Bodleian's *Specimens of Shakespeariana* (new ed. 1927). But we are here concerned with lists which within their scope aim at being exhaustive. The one man who, greatly daring, has attempted the feat of producing a full Shakespeare bibliography, is Capt. William

Jaggard, of Stratford-on-Avon; his volume, *Shake-speare Bibliography*, was published at Stratford in 1911. It contains a very large mass not only of records of editions of Shakespeare, but of criticisms and the like. Its form is its handicap. It is a plain alphabetical dictionary, as indeed its sub-title calls it; and is totally undigested for ordinary use. For quick reference the alphabet is a valuable instrument, if you know what author you want; but when you look a book up in a bibliography it is not often merely in order to be assured of its existence. More often you wish to find what editions or what criticisms there are on a particular work or phase of a man. How does an alphabetical arrangement help you there?

Without holding it up as perfection I would contrast with Jaggard's bibliography the Shakespeare heading in the Museum General Catalogue. Here you will find the works set out, first collected, then separate, in alphabetical order; after the English editions of each follow translations in alphabetical order of language, and then references to critical works on that play or poem. After all these comes the general Appendix of references to literature not dealing with individual plays; and here too a path is blazed through the jungle by the division of the mass into various subheadings: Bibliography, Biography, Criticism (these two often difficult to separate), Authorship Controversy (formerly

76

Baconian Controversy, until there appeared other and rival candidates for the throne of our literary Nephelococcygia), Centenary Celebrations, Ireland Forgeries, and (term of despair) Miscellaneous. On the whole this does break Jaggard's unwieldy and amorphous heap up into sections, each of which can be at once found, and in a few minutes swept by the eye—at least by the practised eye. Of course, if we were in America and had our catalogues—*horresco referens*—on cards, it would take not minutes but hours.

In 1922 Miss Bartlett's *Mr William Shakespeare*, a description of the quartos and folios, and of contemporary source books, covered this fundamental part of the subject thoroughly.

Shakespeare is (rightly) the first author, as Caxton is (rightly) the first printer, the location and history of every copy of whose works in the original editions, has been recorded by census. The late Sir Sidney Lee described in 1902 all the numerous copies of the First Folio then known; of course more have since appeared, some have vanished, and many have made the Grand Tour. In 1916 Miss Bartlett and Mr Pollard, one bibliographer from each side of the Atlantic, combined in a census of the Quartos.

No other great dramatist has been seriously taken in hand by a bibliographer. Consider Dryden: the Grolier Club had an exhibition of his first editions, in 1900, and published a catalogue; Wheatley's list in the *Cambridge History* is very good in its summary way, and it is a pity that Wheatley, who knew as much as any man of Dryden, never did a full-dress bibliography. Recently Mr Wise in his catalogue of his library has given us excellent descriptions of his Drydens, and both he and Mr Percy Dobell, the bookseller, who specialises in the Restoration[1], have done much to disentangle the confusing editions and issues of his books. These are surprisingly numerous; of several of his plays there are two editions of the first year, either (at sight) possibly the first, and only on collation distinguishable at all. Moreover there is a variant issue of *Annus Mirabilis* (not a play, but I mention it here), the earliest of three states of the first edition, which was recorded and cited by Mr John Sargeant in his edition of Dryden, but of which no copy can be found. Every copy of this book that turns up should be closely examined. But I dealt with this point before.

Dryden, of whom there is (astonishingly) not only no good bibliography, but also no good edition, is, I understand, being taken in hand (at least as regards his text) by Mr Montague Summers.

English fiction is less important before 1700 than English drama, and contains more foreign in-

[1] *John Dryden: bibliographical memoranda.* 1922.

fluence. But it includes the first book printed in the English language, *The Recuyell of the Histories of Troy*, at one end of its first two centuries, and the *Pilgrim's Progress* at the other; while in the last two centuries the scales have tipped heavily that way, and more both of talent and of genius have gone to the novel than to the drama.

It fell to me in my earlier days to dig out of all the sources I could think of the English tales and romances printed before 1740—that being the date at which I had been informed that the English novel was born; its ante-natal state proved to have been of a singular vitality, for, as recorded in the volume which the Bibliographical Society published in 1912, it runs to some thousands of titles. This list was divided into two parts, the first containing all editions to 1740 of all books first published before 1640; and the second all editions to 1740 of all books first published in the century between 1640 and 1740. The break, that made by the Civil War, is a real one; there was a cessation of romance-publishing, as of play-acting, the Elizabethan schools of Lyly, Sidney, Greene and Lodge, and the imitations of *Amadis* and *Palmerin* die away; while the French romances of D'Urfé, Gomberville, La Calprenède and Scudéry have barely begun to be translated, and still less had the anti-romances they generated. Only two or three authors actually occur in both parts. The

79

Museum has collected a good number of English romances and novels in the last fourteen years, since this list exhibited the gaps, especially the mid-seventeenth century translations from the long French romances of the Scudéry school. But it is still weak in the chapbook reprints of the popular books like the *Seven Champions of Christendom* and Emmanuel Forde's *Parismus*, which now fetch prices too far out of proportion to their real value to justify the cost of collection. The Bodleian is very rich, especially in just this last class. I am conscious that after 1640, where Sayle's catalogue stops, I did not search U.L.C. properly. When I confessed this to Sayle, he put me to shame by replying that to ignore U.L.C. was traditional and doubtless correct.

A Committee of the Modern Language Association of America has taken up an ambitious single-handed beginning made by Mr John Clapp, and purposes to make a complete bibliography of English fiction from 1700 to 1800. Personally I should make the latter date 1814, when *Waverley* changed English fiction more than *Pamela* had three-quarters of a century earlier. It is perhaps not for me to suggest that the starting-point might as well be 1740 as 1700. I have, however, heard very little lately of this project, and it may be quiescent or even defunct, though I hope not. It will probably appear that the great libraries are

very weak in the minor novels of the later eighteenth century, the products of the Minerva Press
and the like, which enshrine the refined domestic
novel of the Burney type and the early romantic
and historical novel started by Horace Walpole.

Some other special forms of literature have been
treated, translations into English from Greek and
Latin classics before 1641 by Miss Henrietta
Palmer in 1911 (Bibliographical Society), and
those from the Italian (a very important class) in
1895–9, revised in 1916, by Mrs Mary Augusta
Scott (Boston), including some Shakespearean and
other "source-books". Character-books have been
recently and well described by Miss Gwendolen
Murphy. Editions of the Bible are recorded in
various places; notably in Darlow and Moule's
Catalogue of the Bible House Collection, including
many of Francis Fry's copies. Many classes are
left to be done. Miss Bertha Haven Putnam has
recently published a book and incidentally a
bibliography on the fifteenth and sixteenth century
treatises for Justices of the Peace. George Dunn,
having been called to the Bar in his youth, must
needs collect them—as he collected the literature
or specimens of whatever else interested him,
from clocks and telescopes to strange wines, and
in everything he touched he advanced knowledge.
His early law books were bought entire for Harvard, where probably is the finest collection of

English law books to be found anywhere, not excepting the Museum and the Inns of Court. Mr J. H. Beale's *Bibliography of Early English Law Books* (to 1600), 1926, is based on the Harvard collection. But large gaps in English law remain. Nor is there a thorough bibliography of any branch of science to cover any period, nor a good one even of that most popular subject, gardening; while the nearest to one on agriculture is a recent catalogue of the not at all complete library of the Rothamsted Experimental Station. It is, by the way, only three or four years since the national library acquired a copy of the first English printed farming book, FitzHerbert's *Boke of Husbandry* (Pynson, [1523]). English medical, chemical, or mathematical books must be sought in such general repertories as the Catalogue of the Surgeon-General's Library (U.S.A.), 1880, etc., John Ferguson's *Bibliotheca Chemica*, 1906, Zeitlinger and Sotheran's *Bibliotheca Chemico-Mathematica*, 1921, and Augustus de Morgan's *Arithmetical Books*, 1847. Most branches of sport are well covered. All these are literature in the large sense.

The most remunerative genre of all would undoubtedly be non-dramatic verse. No doubt it is the number and the rarity of the books in the early period that have deterred the adventurer; and it could only be done by taking a small field, say up to 1556, at a time. For the early period we have now the Bibliographical Society's *Short Title Catalogue* to pillage for special lists of this and other sorts. That indeed is what it exists for. The sonnet has been pretty well worked out, but we have other forms, the pastoral, pastoral-tragical, tragical-historical, and the rest. A number of the general bibliographies and the private collections I have mentioned or shall mention elsewhere are specially and explicitly devoted to our early poetry.

And after 1640 we shall shortly have in the next short-title catalogue of the Museum (taken with the *Term Catalogues* and the other sources) a groundwork for special lists and studies of the later seventeenth century. The drama has been done (and to speak lightly, I shall not be sorry if the drama gets a good long rest, and students turn to something else). Non-dramatic verse from 1641 to 1700 would shew several things; the rise of the couplet and of the pseudo-Pindaric stanza, the rise and fall of metaphysical poetry, the popularity of satire (natural to a generation wearied by over-strained idealism), the first hymns other than metrical psalms, forerunning Isaac Watts and the Wesleys, the immediate recognition of Milton, who is commented on as a classic by Addison, and of Butler, who fathers the best verse of Swift.

One more class, and not a very literary one, may be worth a few words, and that is the ballad. Not of course the romantic Border ballad, which hardly got into print till modern times (with the exception of *Adam Bell* and one or two more); the ballad I mean is the contemporary set of verses, to a well-known tune, printed on single sheets and hawked by pedlars. They were often pasted on doors and walls of houses, and some have been recovered from under later wall papers. They are sometimes tales of rustic wooings, some indeed are ribaldry; many record hangings, murders, monstrous births, floods and fires, and in fact were the parents of the newspaper.

These single sheets are naturally of great rarity; less so after the middle of the seventeenth century, since there were by that time two or three great collectors of them, such as Pepys and Narcissus Luttrell.

Ballads of the sixteenth century only exist (in more than stray specimens) in four collections. These are the Museum, the Bodleian, the Society of Antiquaries, and the Huntington Library at San Gabriel in California.

The earliest survivors are those at Burlington House; they were catalogued by Robert Lemon in 1866; no fewer than forty-six are pre-Elizabethan. Those of the Museum and at San Gabriel have a curious history. They were originally one bundle of about a hundred and fifty sheets, and belonged to the housekeeper at Helmingham Hall in Suffolk; she sold them to a postmaster, who sold them to a dealer, who sold them to Daniel, who sold half to Heber, which went into the Britwell collection, while the other half went after Daniel's death into Henry Huth's library. This latter collection was transcribed and edited in 1867 (for the Philobiblon Society), and the originals ultimately came as part of Alfred Huth's bequest into the Museum; the twin half went at one of the Britwell sales and is now in the Huntington Library at San Gabriel. These latter were printed in 1912 in an edition by Mr Herbert Collmann, which was presented by Mr Christie-Miller to the Roxburghe Club.

Of the mid and later seventeenth century ballads, great collections exist in the Museum (Roxburghe, Luttrell, Thomason, etc.), Bodleian, Pepys, Haigh Hall, and Manchester Public Library. An American student, Mr Hyder Rollins, has recently published a series of rather haphazard but well-edited selections from these collections; he has also made a valuable contribution to the systematic knowledge of the ballad by a thorough *Analytical Index to the Ballad Entries (1557 to 1709) in the Registers of the Company of Stationers of London* (Univ. of N. Carolina, 1924).

With the exception of periodical miscellanies like the *Spectator*, newspapers did not themselves until recent times (and only sparsely then) contain anything that could aspire to be called literature; but they were early of importance for the announcements they contained of new books, by which much exact information of dates, and sometimes of authorship, is preserved. There are few considerable collections of old newspapers. The Museum has Charles Burney's collection; but there is no special printed catalogue of it; the titles are accessions to the General Catalogue. The Bodleian, on the other hand, printed a catalogue of its periodicals so long ago as 1878–80. There are two general bibliographies; in 1920 *The Times* celebrated the tercentenary of English journalism by publishing a hand-list; and in 1927 Professors R. S. Crane and F. B. Kaye produced *A Census of British Newspapers and Periodicals, 1620–1800*, shewing which are preserved in American libraries; this work is being revised for a second edition.

BIBLIOGRAPHIES OF RELIGIOUS BODIES

Besides literary forms, there are other classes. Notable is the bibliography of a religious body. Certain of the Catholic orders are well provided, as the Jesuits with Sommervogel, and with Uriarte and De Backer; but these only touch English Jesuits incidentally. The greatest source of English Catholic literature is undoubtedly Joseph Gillow's *Bibliographical Dictionary of the English Catholics*, 5 vols. (1885–1902), in which each writer has appended

86

a list of his works, but without bibliographical detail. The extreme rarity of the books—well brought out by Gillow—has stood in the way of any bibliography. The books were often printed abroad, and smuggled over in small editions, of which many copies were destroyed by authority or by private controversialists. A chronological bibliography of these books would be of great value; but it would be an enormous labour and involve touring round the Catholic colleges of England and Ireland, and foreign libraries, and also it would involve a close typographical study of the presses of St Omer, Douai, and elsewhere, at a time when the printer could get ready-made from Antwerp a stock of types and ornaments from the same punches as those of printers else-where. The Catholic Record Society and the Farm Street Fathers, notably Father C. A. Newdigate, are meanwhile the chief repositories of knowledge.

The most important existing bibliography of an English religious body is certainly Joseph Smith's *Descriptive Catalogue of Friends' Books*, 1867–93. The Quakers very early took an interest in their literature, and John Whiting in 1708 published a *Catalogue of Friends' Books*. Based in the main on the Devonshire House Library, Smith's *Catalogue* is, like Gillow's *Dictionary*, biographical in plan. But the biography counts for less, and the bibliography for more. Smith followed it up with a *Bibliotheca Antiquakeriana*, 1873. These two works ought certainly to be combined into a single chronological list (distinguishing the Anti's, if you will, by an asterisk or any other mark of the beast); this would get into order all the controversies, in which some Friends, not wholly exempt from worldly failings, delighted, and shew the literature of both sides. It is also not easy to see one's way through Smith in a big heading like George Fox or William Penn. Unless one knows the dates of the first editions, one does not know whether to turn forwards or backwards. But with these limitations Joseph Smith is excellent. His titles are full and his accuracy of statement worthy of Quaker principles.

Congregationalists also have an important historical list, H. M. Dexter's *Congregationalism of the last three centuries as seen in its Literature*, 1880.

BIBLIOGRAPHIES OF SINGLE AUTHORS

Bibliographies, small or large, bad or good, have been made of a very large number of individual authors, perhaps of all who are of much credit and renown, and certainly of many who are of little; the standard edition of the author is generally a likely place to look in for his bibliography. There would be no possible use in producing a list— even a *catalogue raisonné*—of all or even the best of these; and the more so that Northup's new *Register* (to which I shall recur) is primarily arranged under the names of the authors treated, and is on this side reasonably adequate, if not very critical; and also that Mr Seymour de Ricci, in his *Book-Collectors' Guide*, is careful to mention under each author's name any existing bibliography of his writings. But these author-bibliographies differ not only in size and competence, but also in fundamental plan and idea, and some more remarks are necessary.

A very striking feature of the art is that it is practically the creation of the last or last two generations. The oldest bibliographies of English authors that occur to me are William Lee's of Defoe and George Offor's of Bunyan. But these, while being valuable pieces of research (especially Lee's in the attribution to Defoe of his fugitive pamphlets, from the evidence of the journals and other documents of the time) make no effort at the modern contribution of book-description towards the textual criticism of the original editions. Nor, so late as 1908, does W. Spencer Jackson's bibliography of the eighteenth century editions of Swift, which occupies most of the twelfth and last volume of Swift's *Prose Works*. This last is also a good example of a merit, and of a defect. Jackson tells you where there is a copy of each edition to be found. On the other hand he entirely ignores manuscripts, which for Swift, who took no care in publishing, are many and vital. Nor, while classing genuine and doubtful works separately, does he give reasons for his canon. But Swift's love of mystery, and the freedom with which he was imitated, make this a very necessary task for his bibliographer.

Comparatively few bibliographers have thought it worth while to record the critical and bio-graphical work which has been done on their author. Jaggard's *Shakespeare* does this, and so do the "topical" bibliographies of Chaucer, Spenser and Milton, to which I shall recur. The Shake-speare and Chaucer Allusion Books carry one side of the bibliography of criticism to the furthest stage possible. The fashions of collectors make the necessary financial opportunity for bibliographers, and the original editions are accordingly the common quarry.

This fashion is now for the authors of the eighteenth and nineteenth centuries. The collec-tors who only run after the first editions of the latest authors (having, one supposes, read no others) do not command much respect. But they are part of a salutary revolt against the tyranny of pre-Restoration collecting. Fortunately there is no

need for either narrowness. The great eighteenth
century writers are now mostly provided, Courtney
and Nichol Smith's *Johnson*, 1915, being perhaps
the best. The latest is Griffith's *Pope*, which is
still incomplete, based largely on the Wrenn collection in the University of Texas. For Defoe and
Swift, who are of almost intolerable difficulty,
there exist, beside the lists by Lee and Jackson
already mentioned, minute studies of the earliest
editions of *Robinson Crusoe* by Mr Hubbard, and
of *Gulliver* by Mr Harold Williams, the latter
having appeared in the *Library*. The most magnificent bibliography of an author ever produced is
Dr Keynes's of Blake, issued to members of the
Grolier Club some four years ago. But Blake is *sui
generis*, and it is appropriate that his bibliography
should be so too.

The master, almost the founder, of the collecting
and the consequent bibliography of the nineteenth
century poets is Mr Thomas James Wise, whose
only predecessor, Richard Herne Shepherd, is not
very trustworthy, and has been superseded.
Buxton Forman's bibliography of Keats is a monument of what I may perhaps be allowed to call the
pre-Wise period which is still standard. Mr Wise
has published bibliographies, containing elaborate
book descriptions, of Shelley, Tennyson, Swinburne,
and other poets, based on his own noble collection,
of which I must make further mention in its place.

There is one point I should like to mention in passing. The magazines have added a new terror to bibliography, for the first appearances of most of the shorter works of modern authors have been made in them. The boasted indices to periodicals fail us hopelessly. In recording these first appearances, when found, may I recommend a device I employed when very young in making a bibliography of George Meredith, and which I have not noticed elsewhere? This is to index the poems (in another author it might be tales or essays), not only in the text, but also individually in tabular form, keeping a column for each period between the years of publication of collective volumes, and entering the year of appearance of the single poems in that column.

And further I would deprecate the practice of burdening bibliographies of modern authors with references to trivial reviews. An idea of the reception of a book can be got as well from half-a-dozen as from twenty of the hurried verdicts of Fleet Street.

Bibliography, conceived as a mere list of books and articles, however skilfully drawn up, has been raised to a higher power both of value and of difficulty by the publication in 1908 by Miss Eleanor Prescott Hammond of her *Chaucer: a bibliographical manual*, the first work of the new analytical or topical type. The manuscripts and

the editions are analysed as well as simply classified; thus each poem occurring in either will be
recorded in the section devoted to that particular
poem as so occurring. And the same is done with
critical works. Each chapter or substantial passage
dealing with a work or an aspect of the poet is
separately entered. The whole of Chaucer literature is in this way indexed, and the result is a
sort of encyclopaedia of Chaucerian knowledge.
The book begins with an analysis of the writings
on the life of Chaucer, shewing the supersession of
the legend by accumulating facts, and quoting the
more important from Leland down. Then follow
the canon, the chronology, the sources, and a list
of collected editions; *The Canterbury Tales*; Other
works, alphabetically; Linguistics and Versifica-
tion; Verse and Prose printed with the work of
Chaucer is of the nature of an appendix. The last
section is "Bibliographical", and is not really up
to the rest, consisting of rather meagre practical
hints. There is an excellent index.

The chapter dealing with the minor works is
headed by complete accounts of manuscripts and
editions. If we pick out a poem we shall see the
method. *Bukton* is a simple case. We have first a
note of the sole manuscript and the exact prints
from that manuscript by the Chaucer Society; for
textual notes there are references to *Anglia* and
Englische Studien.

93

Next comes a summary list of the *Editions*, mostly of the *Works*, which contain *Bukton*; then of modernisations and translations wherever found, with references to other sections of the book where modernisations and translations are recorded together.

Authenticity (often no easy matter) is here dealt with by the simple note that the poem is marked as Chaucer's by the manuscript.

A note on the *Title* gives occasion for an account of the variations of title that have been given to the poem (in the teeth of that in the manuscript), and the shiftings it has endured in the editions, from the end of *The Book of the Duchess*, to which Urry (apparently misunderstanding Stow) had regarded it as an envoy, into the Minor Poems, back again, and then again, and finally, into the Minor Poems.

For the *Date* we have three references, to passages in Furnivall's *Trial Forewords*, to Koch's *Chronology*, and to a communication by Skeat to the *Academy*.

Finally *Notes*, referring, for general comment on the poem, to *Notes and Queries*, Morley's *English Writers*, ten Brink, Root's *Poetry of Chaucer*, and Skeat's big edition of Chaucer.

You will perceive that to make a bibliography on these lines you have not merely to record, but to digest and to analyse the literature. *Bukton* is merely a single piece among the Minor Poems; there is no separate edition of it, and no separate work devoted to it. In no ordinary bibliography therefore should we find any mention of it whatever. That Morley, ten Brink, and the others give a couple of pages apiece to it would be buried knowledge, for their books would not be entered at all; Root's *Poetry of Chaucer* would presumably be entered once, but with little or no information as to its contents.

The only drawback to the topical bibliography is the enormous labour needed to produce it, especially for a classic. The class is accordingly very small. Wells's *Manual of the Writings in Middle English* is compiled on the same method; but the only two other similar bibliographies of specific authors are Professor Frederick Ives Carpenter's *Reference Guide to Edmund Spenser*, 1923, and Elbert Thompson's *John Milton: a topical bibliography*, 1916. It is perhaps significant that all four of these works come from America, that spacious land, where Universities have staffs large enough to allow them some leisure.

Carpenter's book is not quite so closely or so well divided as Miss Hammond's. Editions, complete and partial, are disposed of before the sections for his sources, publishers, and pictorial illustrations, begin; and these in turn are followed by sections of general reference for each poem.

95

But the editions of Spenser are much simpler than those of Chaucer, and there are few manuscripts. The plan seems adequate to the matter, which only occupies some three hundred uncrowded pages. In a larger work the alphabetical arrangement of authors of criticisms, etc., especially under *Faerie Queene*, would have been very clumsy.

Thompson's *John Milton* is a still slighter book; and can only be regarded as selective. For example, he only gives exactly fifty entries for general criticism on *Paradise Lost*, and when one considers the mass that has been written upon that celebrated performance, one is perhaps thankful. The arrangement inside each section is chronological, which is much better than the alphabetical, adopted by Carpenter.

None of these three bibliographers indulges in the other form of analytical bibliography, that opposed to systematic, which analyses the physical as well as the literary composition of a volume. They offer no "standard descriptions". This omission is not important, because the books they record have nearly all been already adequately described on the typographical side elsewhere.

But when one thinks of it, every classical author ought to be the matter of a topical bibliography. Shakespeare certainly needs it. The result would be a Shakespeare encyclopaedia; and if the selection were ruthlessly carried out, it would be one of the most valuable books imaginable. Indeed what we have to fear is the unintelligent ambition of a mechanical completeness, which is a specially modern danger.

Another author who would enormously repay work on these lines is Swift. But to set the canon and the text of Swift in order is as great a labour or greater than to do the same for Defoe. The first printed editions are often of low authority, and for large numbers of pieces there are rival manuscripts. I merely suggest these two as remote Himalayan peaks for the bibliographer to conquer. Whoever attempts to apply the topical or analytical method to any considerable author must be ready with "il lungo studio e il grande amore" (justly claimed by Miss Hammond on her title-page), to support him through years of toil.

DICTIONARIES OF ANONYMA
AND PSEUDONYMA

Besides the books with authors, there are the books with none, or with false authors; and to record and find if possible the true attribution is obviously an important side of bibliography, and one which goes far beyond ordinary bibliographical methods into contemporary printed or docu mentary sources.

There is, however, no branch of literary history so ill-served. The standard book, commonly known as "Halkett and Laing", has had a curious history. Samuel Halkett, Librarian to the Advocates, began collecting material in the middle of the last century. He died in 1871 with nothing published; Jamieson, his successor, took over the material; he died in turn, and the Rev. John Laing took it up, but also died before anything was ready for publication. The book was brought out in 1882–8 by his daughter, Catherine Laing, as *A Dictionary of the Anonymous and Pseudonymous Literature of Great Britain.*

The work is very imperfect. Much fuller authority for the attributions should be given. Yet there is nothing in English that so nearly approaches Barbier and Quérard in French. In default of a better Halkett and Laing is the chief and first book of its kind.

The late Dr Kennedy collected much knowledge for a revision and enlargement of the book. But he also died. The publishers have recently revived his project, and have commissioned my colleagues, Mr William Allan Smith (also a Scotsman) and Mr A. Forbes Johnson, to carry it through. Vols. I-II, for which they have little responsibility, have now appeared. The earlier history of the book suggests the Hope Diamond or the fatal mummy, but I hope that Mr Smith and Mr Johnson may survive.

Simultaneously with this there has appeared a similar but comparatively unimportant work by C. A. Stonehill and others. It is a pity that two books, intended for the same small public, should be published at the same time. This was the fate of the original Halkett and Laing. In 1885-8 William Cushing, an American bibliographer, published his *Initials and Pseudonyms* and in 1889 his *Anonyms*. The later of these two books habitually cites the earlier in evidence, but that is the only authority ever given, and except for modern American writers Cushing is of no value whatever.

PRIVATE LIBRARIES AND SALES

Libraries, public and private, in this country which contain incunabula are entered in a handy list by Dr Ernst Crous, of Berlin, who made a census of copies for the purpose of the Gesamtkatalog der Wiegendrucke. Dr Crous read papers to the Bibliographical Society; and his list was published in the *Transactions* in vol. XII, 1914. The libraries, public and private, there entered number 371, and though one would have to use it with discretion, there is no doubt that libraries known to contain incunabula may well also contain old and rare English books. Until the appearance of the directory of special libraries and of special collections in general libraries which Mr Barwick is compiling for the Association of Special Libraries, Dr Crous's list is the best general list to take as a starting point for a search. With it may be compared that in the *Short Title Catalogue of English Books printed before 1640*.

For American libraries there is Dr G. P. Winship's *Census of Fifteenth Century Books owned in America*, 1919, which can be used with just the same reservation.

Two other books may be used as a guide to libraries, public and private, possessing or having possessed English books of mark. These are Mr De Ricci's *Census of Caxtons* and Miss Bartlett's and Mr Pollard's *Census of Shakespeare's Plays in Quarto*, both of which have already been mentioned. Each contains a full index of the owners, with notes of sales, incorporation in public libraries and the like, by which the migrations of copies can be traced.

Book auctions from their beginning in this country have been I suppose nearly exhaustively recorded in the *List of Catalogues of English Book Sales now in the British Museum*, 1915, arranged chronologically and provided with an index of owners (whose names have often had to be supplied, being suppressed by the auctioneers). This great accumulation is of course by no means given over to libraries rich in English books. The sump-

tuous collections of incunabula and foreign litera-
tures, and the insignificant sales of common books,
are all there. But though the really determined
hunter may have to turn to minor catalogues, I
think it is all I can do here if I give a rapid summary of a few of the chief libraries yielding the
"gibier de nostre estude".

The book auction-room has its romance as well
as its squalor, but for that I must refer you to the
writings of Dibdin, John Hill Burton and Andrew
Lang.

In this chronological survey I will include the
chief collections of this kind which now form part
of public, university or collegiate libraries, and so
are stationary and permanent, those which still
exist in private hands, and of which we have
either printed catalogues or some legitimate public
knowledge, and those which have been through
the sale room, and of which the auctioneer's
catalogue is often the sole monument. Of all
these classes there are American as well as English
examples. A unique book in a University Library
in the United States is, in accessibility for English
students, much nearer to one in an English University Library than is one in some English country
house, perhaps in the possession of the collector's
ignorant heirs or descendants, who take no care
of the old library and guard it by admitting no
one, whether scholar or charwoman. Such was

the fate of a certain Chaucer manuscript of my acquaintance until recent years. The Countess who owned it till 1915 refused the Chaucer Society permission to print it in their series of texts; yet in that library I had my only encounter with a live bookworm. There is really not much to lament if important texts leave these remote fastnesses for large and well-organised libraries in America, where there are bibliographers to publish catalogues, to answer our questions with the trained patience of their breed, and to send us collations and photostats that are all but as good as the book itself. And I would remind you that American book-collecting has passed through the first phase, that of mere private hoarding for fashion's sake. Practically all the collectors of to-day have in being or in intention some foundation, like the San Gabriel Library or the Elizabethan Club of Yale, to which their spoils from the sale-room are destined. Occasionally a real corner-stone, like the Ellesmere Chaucer, goes, and the most stoical is moved; but ordinarily we can leave to the newspapers the jeremiads about the American peril.

To turn then to the collections (some of which have already been mentioned); I will give them roughly in the order of their formation:

The small but priceless collection of poetry of the end of the sixteenth century, found in an attic at LAMPORT HALL (I) in the 'sixties by Charles

Edmonds and mostly divided in 1893 between Wakefield Christie Miller of Britwell and the British Museum.

The BRIDGEWATER or ELLESMERE LIBRARY (2), founded by Sir Thomas Egerton at the end of the sixteenth century, and added to in the seventeenth, of which a few rarities were catalogued by John Payne Collier in a limited edition (1837); Collier, with Lord Francis Egerton's permission, incorporated this in 1865 into his *Bibliographical and Critical Account of the Rarest Books in the English Language*. The whole splendid library was bought by Mr Huntington in 1917 and is now (duplicates having been turned out) at San Gabriel in California.

The GORDONSTOUN Library (3), collected in Scotland in the first half of the sixteenth century by Sir Robert Gordon of Gordonstoun; sold in 1816. Rich in early Scottish books.

Robert BURTON (4) bequeathed many English books to the Bodleian and Christ Church; his farming books he left to Mistress Fell, and where are they? The recent list of those at Oxford, published by the Oxford Bibliographical Society, I have already mentioned. Burton's books are of his own day, and are either very scientific or very popular.

George THOMASON's Civil War Tracts (5), now in the British Museum, I have already described.

103

A little later than Burton, Samuel PEPYS (6) collected (unlike Burton or anyone before him) early English books, and also "Penny Merriments", "Penny Godlinesses", and ballads, as well as more literary matter. The present home of this collection, which is the fruit of his admirable intellectual curiosity, is Pepys's (and my own) College, Magdalene. The catalogue of his library I have already mentioned.

Narcissus MARSH (7), Archbishop of Armagh (died 1713), who founded the library at Dublin which bears his name, including Stillingfleet's books. The Bibliographical Society published a list of Marsh's English books before 1640.

John BAGFORD (8), called, probably without justice, the biblioclast, whose collection of ballads, sheets and title-pages went largely into the collection of Harley, and being somehow classed as manuscript (Bagford's manuscript material for his *History of Printing* was there too) came to the Museum.

Narcissus LUTTRELL (9) (died 1732) collected, like Thomason, the fugitive literature of his own day, and marked the day on which he bought each piece and the price. His library was sold in 1786, and divided between Farmer and Bindley. Many of his books came ultimately to the Museum or went to Britwell.

Tom HEARNE (10), the antiquary, whose manuscripts were left by Richard Rawlinson to the

Bodleian. His printed books were sold in 1736 by Osborne.

The HARLEYS (11), Robert and Edward, Earls of Oxford. The great strength of the Harleian library was in English history. After the second earl's death in 1741, the printed books were sold to Osborne, the bookseller, who employed Oldys and Johnson to make the catalogue which appeared in 1744–5. The manuscripts, as is well known, came to the Museum.

Joseph AMES (12), author of the *Typographical Antiquities*; his books were sold in 1760.

Bryan FAIRFAX (13), died 1749; in 1756, his library, catalogued for sale was bought privately by his relative Francis Child of Osterley, and in 1885 the Earl of Jersey sold the library in which they were included. Amongst other books he owned the only perfect copy of the 1485 Malory, which went to Mrs Norton Q, Pope, to Robert Hoe, and at his sale to Pierpont Morgan.

Thomas RAWLINSON (14), died 1725. His vast collection was sold partly in his lifetime and partly after his death in eleven sales from 1721 to 1734. He had twenty-five Caxtons; and it was noted that the English antiquities went dearer than *editiones principes* of the classics, hitherto held in more esteem.

His brother Richard RAWLINSON (15), died 1755, bequeathed his extraordinary collection of historical manuscripts to the Bodleian; early English poetry is represented among them. His printed books were sold in 1757.

James WEST (16), died 1772. He had forty Caxtons, and numbers of other early English books, many of which are now in the Museum; and he started the collection of seventeenth century ballads which became the Roxburghe, and came at the Bright sale in 1845 to the Museum.

Edward CAPELL (17); gave his play-books to Trinity in 1779; catalogue by Dr Greg, 1903.

William HERBERT (18), editor of the *Typographical Antiquities*, died 1795. The great collection of books at Cheshunt, on which he based his revision of Ames, was sold in 1796; Herbert's signature is a well-known and welcome sight to bibliographers. Many of his books were subsequently bought by Heber.

Richard FARMER (19), Master of Emmanuel as well as University librarian, and author of the *Essay on the Learning of Shakespeare*, died 1797. His books were sold in 1798, and are by no means only dramatic. His signature, like Herbert's, is familiar, with the advantage of being a work of art as well as a certificate.

George STEEVENS (20), the Shakespearean scholar, and Isaac REED (21), whose dramatic libraries were sold in 1800 and 1807.

Thomas PARK (22), editor of *Nugae Antiquae* and

literary antiquary (died 1834). His collection of
poetry together with the library of Hill were catalogued by A. F. Griffiths in 1815 for Longmans,
the booksellers, as *Bibliotheca Anglo-poetica*. Other
collections of his were sold in 1826 and 1835.

William BECKFORD (**23**), author of *Vathek*, and
builder of Fonthill, died 1844; some of his library
was sold between 1804 and 1823; but by far the
choicer portion passed through his daughter to
the Dukes of Hamilton, who sold it, with the
Hamilton collection, when Hamilton Palace was
dismantled in 1882–4. This library contained the
finest Blakes but those of Disraeli; several were
bought by Mr B. B. MacGeorge and were sold two
or three years ago.

John Ker, Duke of ROXBURGHE (**24**), died 1804;
his magnificent collection was sold in 1812,
and made a sensation by the high prices which
were paid. It was not specialised, like Reed's or
Herbert's, but was cosmopolitan and English,
learned and popular, literary and typographical
at once. The sale gave birth, as is well known, to
the Roxburghe Club, and also incidentally to the
useful word *uniquity*, which occurs in the catalogue.
The catalogue is classified, and, like most sale
catalogues till later than this, very brief.

The topographical and antiquarian collections
of Richard GOUGH (**25**) (died 1809) were bequeathed to the Bodleian.

James BINDLEY (26), Commissioner of Stamp Duties, died 1818. His library, sold in 1818–21, was rich in early English books, especially Elizabethan and Jacobean literature, and contained a quantity of Narcissus Luttrell's late seventeenth-century ballads and political sheets.

Edmund MALONE (27), the Shakespeare commentator, died 1815; his best books (not all plays) were presented to the Bodleian in 1816 by his brother, Lord Sunderlin. The catalogue of them was published in 1836.

Francis DOUCE (28), author of the *Illustrations of Shakespeare* and Keeper of Manuscripts at the British Museum, resigned owing to a disagreement with a Trustee, and, dying in 1834, bequeathed his collection of books (not only English) and illuminated manuscripts to the Bodleian. The Catalogue was published in 1840, and the books in it are not covered by the Bodleian General Catalogue of 1843–51.

Sir Mark Masterman SYKES (29), died 1823. His library, sold in 1824, is chiefly famous for its incunabula, which included copies of the 42-line Bible and the Psalter of 1459; but he also had a quantity of English books of the fifteenth, sixteenth and seventeenth centuries; many found their way to Britwell.

The scientific library of Sir Joseph BANKS (30) (died 1820) was bequeathed to the British Museum. It is rich in travels.

Richard HEBER (31) collected an enormous library, perhaps the largest ever collected by one man, amounting, it is thought, to about 150,000 volumes, the most valuable part of which consisted of early English poetry. The books in his houses in England were sold in 1834–7 and swamped the market; the cream of the English books were bought by W. H. Miller and became the Britwell library. The nation and the two Universities should have bought Heber's whole library and sold the duplicates; but it seems not to have been thought of; it would have cost them about £15,000 apiece.

George John, Earl SPENCER (32), died 1840, collected the Althorp library of early printed books, which was elaborately catalogued by his librarian, Dibdin, in the *Bibliotheca Spenceriana*, 1814–23; the third volume contains the English books, including the second copy known (wanting eleven leaves) of the 1485 Malory. The whole collection was bought in 1892 by Mrs Rylands for the John Rylands Library, Manchester, and at a stroke caused the name of that prosperous city to be heard of by the learned of other lands. The Spencer books are summarily entered in the general catalogue of the Library, and this is better for reference than Dibdin, since the attributions to dates, presses, etc. were made by Gordon Duff.

Benjamin Heywood BRIGHT (33), whose collection of early English literature was sold in 1844-5, and helped to swell the Britwell, Huth, and other libraries; the Roxburghe ballads came from his sale to the British Museum.

Thomas GRENVILLE (34) outlived his retirement from politics for nearly forty years and died in 1846, bequeathing to the Museum his great library, remarkable for the beauty of the copies and especially rich (for our present purpose) in poetry, romances and travels, but not in plays, which (in spite of the notable copy of the First Folio of Shakespeare) seem not to have attracted him. A special catalogue was published, begun in 1842 by the booksellers Payne and Foss, and completed for the Trustees of the British Museum.

George DANIEL (35) of Canonbury, died in 1864, his books sold the same year. He amassed a great Shakespearean and theatrical collection, and also a surprising quantity of chapbooks, jest books, from *Maid Emlyn* and the *Widow Edith* down, drolleries and the like. His outlook seems to have been humorous and satirical—as indeed his many miscellaneous writings testify—and his library illustrated social life rather than high literature. He owned half the Helmingham ballads, which were (as mentioned above, p. 85), bought at his sale by Henry Huth.

Edward Vernon UTTERSON (36) (died 1856,

sales in 1852 and 1857) like Daniel collected popular literature, but rather with an eye to poetry and romance, in both of which he edited various volumes. He was strong in the poets who were Shakespeare's contemporaries.

William Cavendish, Duke of DEVONSHIRE (37) (died 1858) in 1821 bought the Kemble plays, since 1914 in the Huntington library along with the twenty-five Caxtons from Chatsworth. For the latter, we have the catalogue of 1879 by Sir J. P. Lacaita. There are also in the library the chemical collections of Henry Cavendish, and many seventeenth century books on America, particularly Virginia, collected by the first Earl, one of the "planters" of that colony.

The Rev. Thomas CORSER (38), of Manchester (died 1876), made a very large library of early poetry. There are two catalogues of this: one which he made, elaborately annotated in the Dibdin-Collier fashion, and published in the Chetham Society's *Miscellany* in eleven volumes (1860–83) under the title *Collectanea Anglo-Poetica*; the other the sale catalogues of 1868–76. The rarities at these sales were nearly all bought for the Huth and Britwell libraries.

Alexander DYCE (39) in 1869 bequeathed to the South Kensington Museum his collection, chiefly rich in Tudor and Stuart drama. A separate catalogue was published in 1875.

John FORSTER (40) also bequeathed his books to South Kensington, and a catalogue appeared in 1888. This library is vital to any student or editor of Swift, Garrick, or Dickens.

The present Lord CRAWFORD's grandfather (41) made a vast and valuable collection of books and manuscripts. His son, the late Lord CRAWFORD, collected more and sold and collected again. He printed in 1910–13 a great general catalogue (*Bibliotheca Lindesiana*), which is followed by special catalogues of ballads and proclamations. The Haigh Hall MSS. are now in the John Rylands Library. Sales from the library, including some of the rarest books, took place in 1887, 1889 and 1896.

The great ASHBURNHAM library (42), chiefly celebrated for very early manuscripts, also contained many fine printed books. Sales in 1897 and 1898 included Caxtons and other early English books and books on fishing, notably a long set of Walton's *Compleat Angler*.

From 1887 on, the confused records of the sale-room have been brought into system, primarily of course for the bookseller, but also incidentally for the bibliographer and student, by the series of annual volumes of *Book Prices Current*. Notes are sparse, and the *Book Prices Current* do not save reference to the original auction catalogues they index; rather they direct it. Each volume is arranged sale by sale, and has an annual index; in later years the titles are arranged alphabetically. But the decennial indices are recommended. The year is the auction-room season. Thus 1925 means October 1924 to July 1925. A rival, *Book Auction Records*, which includes more unimportant books, was started in 1903; it also has decennial indices.

American Book Prices Current, on the same lines, began in 1895 and is still current.

A useful time-saver for hunting up books sold by auction round about 1900 on either side of the Atlantic is Luther S. Livingston's *Auction Prices of Books*, 1905, in which selected contents of the annuals are reduced to a single alphabet.

In the period since the inception of the various *Book Prices Current* two book-sales (or rather series of book-sales) have been held which overshadow all others in their importance for English literature. These are the Huth and the Britwell.

In the third quarter of the nineteenth century Henry HUTH (43) collected manuscripts and printed books of most important kinds, English and foreign, early printed and later, but not modern. After his death, in 1878, his son, Alfred Henry, carried the library on and added a little. The library was catalogued by F. S. Ellis and W. C. Hazlitt in 1880 in five fine volumes, which instantly became a standard work. Alfred Huth bequeathed to the Museum its choice of any fifty books (a form of benefaction that I hope may find followers, now that whole libraries add so little if they have to be kept entire[1]); of this bequest the Trustees published a full catalogue. The remainder of the library was sold between 1911 and 1920 in a series of annual auctions.

Before the Huth sales ceased the BRITWELL (44) sales began, and are now only just over. This library was formed by William Henry Miller of Craigentinny, and was added to till about the end of the nineteenth century, the Mr Christie Miller of the day dividing, for example, with the Museum the wonderful find of Elizabethan poetry from Lamport.

Miller bought enormously at the Heber sales in 1834–7, especially in English poetry, which was his passion. He was only moderately interested in the drama, but he also collected early Scottish books, Americana, early English science, and English romances and travels, neo-Latin and incunabula. About 1873, parts of the catalogue were printed but never published, though a general catalogue was for ever being prepared, first by Mr R. E. Graves, of the Museum, and later by Mr Herbert Collmann. The sales have not followed any single catalogue order, and the catalogues are not easy to consult. To meet this want Mr Collmann has

[1] Except where they provide fine duplicate copies to be preserved for exhibition.

in preparation for Mr S. R. Christie Miller a comprehensive one-line finding-list of the whole—a
unique case, for a man to publish a catalogue of
his library after he has parted with it and not
before, thus erecting, as it were, a tombstone to the
departed.

If you have traced a book to Heber or Daniel
or Utterson, and want to know where it went to,
look in the Huth catalogue and the *Book Prices
Current* of the Britwell years. If it is in the latter
try the Huntington library next, for in these years
Mr Henry Huntington was by far the largest buyer
in the market.

The sale of Lord MOSTYN's collection (45) of
plays in 1919 was mentioned under the bibliography of the drama.

Not all important libraries and collections that
have been sold have gone through the auction-
room and so been recorded in the various annual
Book Prices Current. Frederick LOCKER (46), afterwards Locker Lampson, of Rowfant, collected,
with fine taste rather than with lavish expense, a
most intimate and delightful library of modest
dimensions, rich in Shakespeare, in Blake, and in
most of the poets of the sixteenth and seventeenth
centuries. His catalogue, *The Rowfant Library*
(1886, supplement 1900), was one of Mr Alfred
Pollard's earliest works, and is preluded by two
poems by Andrew Lang.

The Rowfant books were added to after Locker's death, but sold in 1905 to E. D. Church, the American collector. Church sold part of the collection to the New York dealers, Dodd, Mead and Co., and some came back to England, one or two to the Museum, from that bourne whence as a rule no traveller of this kind returns; Church's library was bought entire by Mr Huntington and is now at San Gabriel.

The best collection of English literature still in private hands in this country is certainly that of Mr T. J. WISE (47). Mr Wise began when a young man as a lover of the poets, and carried this simple and honourable passion into practice, collecting the original editions and manuscripts of Shelley, Browning, Tennyson, Swinburne, and the Rossettis, and his special catalogues, such as those of Shelley and Swinburne, are monuments. But he extended his scope, and his last general catalogue, compiled by himself, is a first-rate authority for the works (prose included) of the English poets of the seventeenth, eighteenth and nineteenth centuries.

The library at Dorchester House, rich in Shakespeare quartos—the finest surviving copies, I believe—and some other rare English books, was collected by R. S. HOLFORD (48), largely from Lord Vernon's library, and remained almost unknown: the best of it was privately sold by the late Sir George Holford before his death in 1926.

Of American collections I feel less able to speak. One of the earliest that abounded in English literature was that of Robert HOE (49), the inventor of the rotary steam press. He published catalogues, conveniently divided into authors who flourished before and after 1700. His books were sold in 1911–13; the sale catalogue adds to the earlier ones. Hoe possessed the Osterley Malory, which went later to the Pierpont MORGAN collection (50). Morgan was famous as a collector twenty or thirty years ago, and bought every sort of work of art, were it the finest of its kind. He was the first to sweep Europe irresistibly. In this way he bought William Morris's early printed books, Lord Amherst's seventeen Caxtons, and great numbers of literary manuscripts.

There is no catalogue of any but part of the early printed books in the Morgan Library. The Library is now a public foundation, under a trust, and is still housed in the building Morgan built for it in New York.

Three older collections, which have gravitated together (1895) into the NEW YORK PUBLIC LIBRARY (51), are the Astor, Tilden and Lenox. The greater Universities, especially Yale, with its ELIZABETHAN CLUB (52), are now very rich in English; and one of two minor Universities, for instance that of Texas, which has the eighteenth-century library of John H. WRENN (53) (catalogued by Wrenn and Wise) including that of George Aitken.

Important sales have been those of VAN ANT-WERP (**54**), 1907, Herschel V. JONES (**55**), 1918–23, HAGEN (**56**), 1918 (strong in the eighteenth century), J. L. CLAWSON (**57**), books before 1640 (1925) especially a collection of John Taylor the water poet, carefully catalogued by Mr De Ricci a couple of years ago and now sold. But the greatest American collector was, till his death in 1927, Mr Henry E. HUNTINGTON (**58**). I have already mentioned his library several times. His books before 1640 rival the Museum's, and are in his foundation at San Gabriel, near Pasadena in California. Mr Huntington often bought whole libraries (rejecting duplicates afterwards) and largely at all great sales for the last fifteen years. A check-list of what was then there was published in 1919; a full bibliographical catalogue is in preparation. One of the libraries swallowed whole, that of E. D. CHURCH (**59**), already mentioned, was excellently catalogued by Dr G. W. Cole, afterwards Mr Huntington's librarian, and till the Huntington catalogue appears we must use the check-list and the Church, Bridgewater and Devonshire catalogues.

Other important private collections are Mr W. A. WHITE's Shakespearean and Elizabethan collection (**60**), catalogued in 1926 by Miss H C.

Bartlett. Mr White, I like to record, more than once stood aside at auctions, hearing that the British Museum was bidding for a particular volume that he wanted; not all English collectors have this decency.

Mention must also be made of the splendid Johnson collection of Mr Robert ADAM (61) of Buffalo, and the smaller but still fine ones of Mr A. Edward NEWTON (62) of Philadelphia and Lt.-Col. Ralph ISHAM (63). Mr Adam has printed a catalogue, which, though not well produced by its printers, is full of facsimiles and very valuable; a revised edition is in preparation. The eighteenth century is indeed now the hunting ground of the collector, and the Americans did not merely, as with the earlier periods, catch us up, but showed more intelligence and started first.

Other American libraries important for English books are those of Mr Charles W. CLARK (64) (catalogued by the owner), of Mr William A. CLARK (65) (catalogued by the owner and recently presented to Los Angeles), of Mr Jerome KERN (66), of the late Mr J. A. SPOOR (67), strong in nineteenth-century literature, of Mr Carl H. PFORZHEIMER (68) (Elizabethan books and Shelleiana), of Mr Owen D. YOUNG (69), and many others.

Some account of recent book-collectors, English and American, was contributed in 1926 by Mr Seymour de Ricci to the *Bulletin du Bibliophile*.

LISTS OF BIBLIOGRAPHIES

Some of the books I have described have been entered in a short classified handlist by Professor Cross of Chicago, which I should like to recommend to you for ready reference[1]. It is classified, and, though too meagre on the one hand, and inclusive of quite irrelevant books on the other, is the best thing of the kind. It is issued interleaved.

A much larger book with the same and other faults, but of much use, is the new *Register of Bibliographies of the English Language and Literature*, 1925, by C. S. Northup.

This substantial work is, like many modern products of American scholarship, almost too laborious. But if you want a bibliography of a particular author or class you can find it there, since the whole is arranged by the alphabetical order of subjects. The general section, however, is unclassified and all but unusable, and there are in it numerous irrelevant books taking up room, as well as an indiscriminate mixture of standard works with trivial and elementary lists. A bad omission is that of sale catalogues, of which few appear.

[1] *A List of Books and Articles, chiefly bibliographical, designed to serve as an introduction to the Bibliography and Methods of English Literary History.* Compiled by Tom Peete Cross (Univ. of Chicago Press, 1919, 3rd ed. 1925).

With all these imperfections the book gives us a new starting-point in this kind of enquiry.

In a rapid survey of so large a subject I have perforce been superficial; nor can I hope that omissions will not be found. Nevertheless I hope that I may have done something to help the inexperienced student to find his way through the vast accumulations of bibliographical sources which confront him, and also to provide him with hints as to where unharvested fields are to be found. Whoever puts his hand to one of these neglected corners is helping to bring into being the complete bibliography of English literature.

ADDENDA

p. 103. For the Lamport books see R. E. Graves in Bibliographica.

p. 105. For the library of George Clark, now at Worcester College, Oxford, see Oxford Bibliographical Society, I. 3.

p. 114. There were Britwell sales in 1910 and 1916, but the main series began later.

p. 119. Mr Jerome Kern's library (66) is about to be sold (1928).

INDEX

l.=library of; other abbreviations will not
need explanation.

INDEX

Commonwealth tracts. *See* Civil War tracts

Congregationalist books, 87

Cooke, J. H., Cheshire bibl., 67

Cooper, C. and T., *Athenae Cantabrigienses*, 65

Copyright Acts, the, 58

Corser, T., l., 111

Cotton, Sir R., 15

Counties, printing in the, 62–9

Courtney, W. P., and Smith, D. N., *Bibliography of S. Johnson*, 91

Coxe, H. O., his catalogues of Oxford MSS., 17

Crane, R. S., and Kaye, F. B., *A Census of British Newspapers and Periodicals*, 86

Crawford, Earls of, l., 112; ballads in, 85

Creswell, S. F., his Nottinghamshire bibl., 67

Cross, T. P., *List of Books and Articles*, 120

Crous, E., his list of English libraries containing incunabula, 99

Cushing, W., *Anonyms*, and *Initials and Pseudonyms*, 99

Dan, P., cancel in his *Histoire de Barbarie*, 8–9

Daniel, G., l., 110; owned the Helmingham ballads, 84

Darien Company, the, J. Scott's coll. and bibl. of, 61

Darlow, T. H., and Moule, H. F., *Catalogue of the Bible House Collection*, 81

Davies, R., *The York Press*, 65

Defoe, D., W. Lee's list of his minor works, 89; L. Hubbard's work on *Crusoe*, 91

De Morgan, A., *Arithmetical Books*, 82

Derbyshire, bibl. by A. Wallis, 67

De Ricci, S., *Book-Collectors' Guide*, 32, 89; *Census of Caxtons*, 42; catalogue of the Clawson Library, 118; account of recent collectors by, 119

Devonshire, Dukes of. *See* Chatsworth

Devonshire press, bibl. of, by J. I. Dredge, 67

Dexter, H. M., *Congregationalism*, 88

Dibdin, T. F., his catalogue of the Spencer Library, 109; his ed. of Ames and Herbert, 41

Dickens, C., Forster coll. of, 112

Dickson, R., and Edmond, J. P., *Annals of Scottish Printing*, 59

Dictionary of National Biography, 24–5

Dix, E. R. McC., his work on Irish books, 62

Dobell, P. J., *John Dryden*, 78

Dorchester House, l., 116

Douce, F., l., 108

Drama, 70–78; MSS. of early, 18. *See* Capell, E.; Chatsworth; Daniel, G.; Douce, F.; Dyce, A.; Farmer, R.; Forster, J.; Garrick, D.; Malone, E.; Mostyn, Lord; Steevens, G.; White, W. A.

Dredge, J. I., Devon bibl., 67

Dryden, J., 77–8

Dublin, Marsh's L., 47–8, 104
— Trinity College Library, General Catalogue of, 29–30; 61

Duff, E. G., *A Century of the English Book Trade*, 68; *Fifteenth Century English Books*, 42–4; *William Caxton*, 42; his cat. of Pepys's *Early English books*, 39, of those in John

INDEX

For EU product safety concerns, contact us at Calle de José Abascal, 56–1°,
28003 Madrid, Spain or eugpsr@cambridge.org.

www.ingramcontent.com/pod-product-compliance
Ingram Content Group UK Ltd.
Pitfield, Milton Keynes, MK11 3LW, UK
UKHW012333130625
459647UK00009B/250